THE One & Only pies and tarts Cookbook

NH
NEW HOLLAND

THE One & Only pies and tarts Cookbook

All the recipes you will ever need

With a Foreword by
Jenny Linford

NEW HOLLAND

First published by New Holland Publishers in 2012
London · Cape Town · Sydney · Auckland

www.newhollandpubishers.com

86 Edgware Road, London W2 2EA, United Kingdom

Wembley Square, Solan Road, Gardens, Cape Town 8001, South Africa

1/66 Gibbes Street, Chatswood, NSW 2067, Australia
www.newholland.com.au

218 Lake Road, Northcote, Auckland 0746, New Zealand

Created by
Pulp Media, Richmond, London

Project Editors: Emma Wildsmith and Helena Caldon
Art Director: Susi Martin
Illustrations: Tracy Turnbull

Photography: Charlotte Tolhurst, Stockfood Ltd, Philip Wilkins: 60-61, 84-85, 128-129, 172-173, 194-195, Shutterstock.com: 1, 2, 6, 10,14, 17, 18, 223, 224-5, 233, 238-239.
Every effort has been made to credit photographers and copyright-holders. If any have been overlooked we will be pleased to make the necessary corrections in subsequent editions.

Publisher: James Tavendale
www.pulp.me.uk

Copyright © 2012 Pulp Media Limited
All rights reserved. No part of this publication may be reproduced, stored in a retrieval system or transmitted, in any form or by any means, electronic, mechanical, photocopying, recording or otherwise, without the prior written permission of the publishers and copyright holders.

A record of this book is available from the National Library.
ISBN 9781742572482
Printed in China
10 9 8 7 6 5 4 3 2 1

"A boy doesn't have to go to war
to be a hero; he can say he doesn't like
pie when he sees there isn't
enough to go around."

Jean-Anthelme Brillat-Savarin

Contents

Foreword

By Jenny Linford

Pastry lends itself to many uses in the kitchen, among them making pies and tarts. Whether you're serving up a hearty meat pie as a main course or rounding off a meal with an elegant sweet tart, pies and tarts are always something of a treat. Although there's a mystique about cooking with pastry, it is, in fact, very simple if you follow a few golden rules. Once you've learnt how to work with pastry, then you can enjoy making a huge range of sweet and savoury pies and tarts, much to the delight of your family and friends.

The golden rules of pastry handling

Keep pastry chilled

Because of its fat content, pastry should be kept chilled until just before using and you should work with it quickly, ideally in a cool kitchen, before it warms up. Equally, when making pies do remember if using a pre-cooked filling, such as braised beef, that it must be **cooled** before you cover it with a pastry lid.

Light Handling

Quick, light handling of pastry produces the best results, as over-handling will make it toughen.

Rolling out

Most types of pastry need rolling out. Roll out your pastry, using a floured rolling pin on a lightly floured surface, with long strokes away from you, rotating the pastry so as to roll it out evenly until it reaches the required size and thickness.

Resting pastry

If making your own pastry, once it's made, be sure to wrap it in cling film and chill it in the fridge for at least half an hour to rest it before using. This simple but important step allows the gluten to develop, making your dough more pliable and less likely to break or shrink. If your pastry has been chilled for longer than half an hour, then bring it out of the fridge and bring it to room temperature 15–20 minutes before rolling in order to allow it to soften and make it easier to handle. Resting a pastry case before baking it is also advisable.

Blind baking

Many recipes for tarts start with a part-baked or whole-baked pastry case made by what is called 'blind baking', a preliminary baking which helps ensure a deliciously crisp pastry shell.

Having rolled out your pastry and lined your flan tin, use a fork to prick the pastry base all over to ensure it doesn't bubble up during baking. Ideally, rest it in the fridge for half an hour. This will reduce the risk of shrinkage when the pastry case is baked.

Line the pastry case with baking parchment and fill it with ceramic baking beans, lentils or rice to weight it down. Bake the pastry case in an oven preheated to 200°C/400°F/gas mark 6 for 15 minutes. Now the case is set, remove the baking parchment and the baking beans and, depending on the recipe, bake it uncovered for 5 minutes for a partly baked case or for 10–15 minutes longer until golden and completely cooked through. You can then fill this pastry case as required.

Making a pie crust

If you're making a single-crust pie (that is a pie with a single piece of pastry covering the filling but no pastry lining), then cut a narrow strip from the rolled pastry, brush this with lightly with water and place this, dampened side-down, round the rim, pressing it onto the dish. Brush with water to dampen it and place the pastry lid over the dish, pressing it onto the dampened pastry strip to seal the pie.

For a double-crust pie (that is a pie with pastry lining and a pastry lid), place the rolled out pastry for the lining in the dish so that it overhangs the edges, brush the pastry edges with water, then place the pastry lid on top, pressing together to seal it, then trim off the excess pastry.

Making your pies and tarts look good

Finish off your tart nicely by working on its pastry edge, crimping them or pressing them evenly with the tines of a fork to make a pattern.

Don't discard your pastry trimmings. Instead, roll them out and use them on your pies to make pastry decorations, such as flowers, hearts or crowns or to write pastry messages. Brush the underside with water or beaten egg, then stick them onto the pie lid. For tarts, use the trimmings to make a decorative pastry edge, such as a plaited onr.

Add an attractive sheen to your pies and tarts by brushing the pastry lightly with milk or, for a rich, glossy golden colour, beaten egg or egg yolk. With a sweet pie, add texture by sprinkling over crunchy sugar, such as Demerara, on top of the glaze.

Pecan tart

1. To make the pastry, sift the flour and salt into a mixing bowl. Rub in the butter using your fingertips until the mixture resembles breadcrumbs. Stir in the sugar until well combined. Stir in the egg yolk and 4 tablespoons cold water until the mixture forms a firm dough. Knead lightly on a lightly floured work surface. Cover with clear film and chill for 30 minutes.

2. Roll the pastry out on a lightly floured work surface and use to line a 25cm round fluted flan tin. Prick the base and sides with a fork, cover and chill for 1 hour. Meanwhile, preheat the oven to 375°F (190°C).

3. Line the pastry case with baking parchment and baking beans, and bake blind for 10 minutes. Remove the beans and paper and bake for a further 5–10 minutes. Remove from the heat.

4. Reduce the oven temperature to 325°F (160°C). Pick out 100g whole, well-formed pecans and set aside. Chop the rest and mix together with the remaining ingredients. Pour into the prepared pastry case. Arrange the whole pecans on top and bake for about 1 hour until the filling is set.

5. Serve warm with scoops of caramel ice cream.

Preparation time: 30 min
 plus chilling
Cooking time: 1 h 15 min
Serves 6–8

For the pastry:
225g plain flour
a pinch of salt
100g butter
25g caster sugar
1 egg yolk

For the filling:
250g pecan halves
3 eggs, beaten
225g light brown sugar
225ml evaporated milk
½ vanilla pod seeds
50g butter, melted

toffee or caramel ice cream, to serve

Mince pies

1. Sift the flour and salt into a mixing bowl. Rub in the butter using your fingertips until the mixture resembles breadcrumbs. Stir in the almonds, egg yolk and 4–5 tablespoons cold water until the mixture forms a firm dough. Knead lightly on a lightly floured work surface. Cover with clear film and chill for 30 minutes.

2. Preheat the oven to 400°F (200°C). Roll out the pastry out on a lightly floured work surface and, using a 7.5cm round fluted cutter, cut 18 circles. Use to line patty tins, pressing the pastry down well. Spoon the mincemeat into the pastry cases. Brush the edges with water.

3. Then, using a 6.5-cm round fluted cutter or any other cutter shape, cut out 18 circles, rerolling any trimmings if necessary. Use to cover the mincemeat, pinching the edges together to enclose. Cut steam holes in the centre and brush the tops with water. Dredge with icing sugar and bake for 20–25 minutes until golden. Serve hot or cold.

Preparation time: 30 min
  plus chilling
Cooking time: 25 min
Serves 18

300g plain flour
a pinch of salt
150g butter
25g ground almonds
1 egg yolk
350g good-quality mincemeat
icing sugar

Treacle tart

1. Place the flour, salt and butter in a food processor and blend until the mixture resembles breadcrumbs. Add the sugar and one of the eggs and blend until the mixture forms a firm dough. Knead lightly on a floured work surface. Cover with clear film and chill for 30 minutes.

2. Roll three-quarters of the pastry out on a lightly floured work surface, and use it to line a 23cm round loose bottomed fluted flan tin. Prick the base and sides with a fork, cover and chill for 30 minutes. Meanwhile, preheat the oven to 375°F (190°C).

3. Line the pastry case with baking parchment and baking beans, and bake blind for 10 minutes. Remove the beans and paper and bake for a further 5–10 minutes. Remove from the heat.

4. Increase the oven temperature to 400°F (200°C). Roll out the remaining pastry on a lightly floured work surface and, using a crinkle pastry cutter, cut out strips.

5. Heat the golden syrup in a saucepan until warm and stir in remaining ingredients until well combined. Pour into the prepared pastry case, level the surface and decorate with lattice pastry, pressing down well on the pastry edge. Beat the remaining egg and brush the pastry strips. Bake for 15 minutes. Reduce oven temperature to 350°F (180°C) and bake for a further 15–20 minutes, until the filling is set. Allow to cool for 15 minutes, before serving.

Preparation time: 30 min
  plus cooling and chilling
Cooking time: 50 min
Serves 6–8

225g plain flour
a pinch of salt
125g butter
1 tbsp caster sugar
2 eggs
400g golden syrup
170g fresh white breadcrumbs
grated rind and juice of 1 lemon

Lemon tart

Preparation time: 20 min
  plus about 3 h cooling
  and chilling
Cooking time: 1 h
Serves 6

For the pastry:
175g plain flour
a pinch of salt
75g butter
25g caster sugar
1 egg yolk

For the filling:
2 eggs, beaten
1 egg yolk
75g caster sugar
juice of 3 lemons
zest of 1 lemon
100ml double cream
blueberries, strawberries and
  icing sugar, to decorate

1. To make the pastry, sift the flour and salt into a mixing bowl. Rub in the butter using your fingertips until the mixture resembles breadcrumbs. Stir in the sugar until well combined. Stir in the egg yolk and 2–3 tablespoons cold water until the mixture forms a firm dough. Knead lightly on a floured work surface. Cover with clear film and chill for 30 minutes.

2. Roll the pastry out on a lightly floured work surface and use to line a 23cm round loose bottomed fluted flan tin. Prick the base and sides with a fork, cover and chill for 30 minutes. Meanwhile, preheat the oven to 375°F (190°C).

3. Line the pastry case with baking parchment and baking beans and bake blind for 10 minutes. Remove the beans and paper, and bake for a further 5–10 minutes. Remove from the heat.

4. Reduce the oven temperature to 275°F (140°C). For the filling, mix together all the ingredients until well blended. Pour into the prepared pastry case and bake for about 35–40 minutes, until filling is set. Allow to cool and chill for 2 hours.

5. Arrange blueberries and strawberries around the edge of the tart and dust heavily with icing sugar.

Banoffee pie

1. Preheat oven to 350°F (180°C).

2. Place the biscuits in a plastic bag and crush with a rolling pin. Melt the butter in a large saucepan and then stir in the biscuits until well coated. Spoon into a 23cm round, loose bottomed, fluted flan tin, pressing down and up the sides of the tin. Chill for 30 minutes.

3. Bake the biscuit base for 10 minutes. Remove from the oven and allow to cool. Spread the caramel over the biscuit base evenly and chill.

4. Unmould the flan and transfer to a serving plate. Arrange the banana slices on top. Whip together the cream and vanilla seeds and spread over the bananas.

5. Cut the chocolate into shards and scatter over the cream.

Preparation time: 20 min
  plus 1 h cooling and chilling
Cooking time: 15 min
Serves 6

225g digestive biscuits
125g butter
1 x 397g can caramel toffee filling
2 bananas, sliced
300ml double cream
½ vanilla pod seeds
50g dark chocolate

Spinach pie with egg

1. For the pastry, sift the flour into a mixing bowl and stir in the salt. Rub in the butter until the mixture resembles breadcrumbs. Gradually add the water, a tablespoon at a time, mixing continuously until the mixture just comes together as a dough. Roll the dough into a ball, then wrap in cling film and chill for 1 hour. Preheat the oven to 400°F (200°C). Grease a 23cm flan tin or dish.

2. For the filling, wash the spinach and cook in a pan with the water just clinging to the leaves, until just wilted. Remove and leave to cool, before chopping roughly. Heat the butter in a pan and add the shallots and spinach. Cook for 10 minutes, then stir in the thyme and pine nuts. Season with salt and pepper. Mix together the milk, cream, egg yolks, flour and cheese.

3. Roll out two-thirds of the pastry on a floured work surface, until it is almost twice as wide as the diameter of the pie tin. Line the base and sides of the tin. Gently press the pastry into the corners of the tin, trimming off any excess. Put half the spinach mixture on the pastry base and arrange the halved eggs on top. Cover with the remaining spinach mixture. Pour in the egg mixture.

4. Roll out the remaining pastry on a floured surface until it is slightly larger than the tin. Brush the rim of the cooked pastry case with some of the whisked egg and place the pastry lid on top of the pie. Trim off any excess pastry.

5. Make two small holes in the centre of the pastry lid. Brush with the remaining beaten egg and bake for 50–60 minutes until golden-brown.

Preparation time: 25 min
 plus 1 h chilling
Cooking time: 1 h
Serves 4

For the pastry:
450g plain flour
a pinch of salt
200g butter
50ml water

For the filling:
900g spinach
2 tbsp butter
2 shallots, chopped
2 tsp chopped thyme
50g pine nuts
100ml milk
100ml cream
2 egg yolks
1 tbsp flour
4 tbsp grated Parmesan cheese
4 hard-boiled eggs, shelled and
 halved lengthwise

To finish:
1 egg, whisked

Tomato and cheese tartlet with basil

1. Preheat the oven to 400°F (200°C). Grease a tart tin.

2. Quickly combine all the pastry ingredients, form into a ball, wrap in cling film and chill for at least 1 hour.

3. Beat the eggs with the cream, crème fraîche and mozzarella and season with a pinch of nutmeg, mustard, lemon zest, salt and ground black pepper. Stir in the basil.

4. Roll out the pastry approximately 3–4 mm thick. Cut out a circle to fit the tart tin and place it in the greased tin. Fill with the egg and cream mixture and place the tomatoes in the mixture with the cut surfaces facing upwards. Bake for about 30 minutes.

5. Remove the quiche from the tin and serve on plates garnished with basil.

Preparation time: 1 h 15 min
  plus 1 h chilling
Cooking time: 30 min
Serves 2

For the pastry:
100g cold butter
200g plain flour
1 egg
1 tbsp basil, finely chopped

For the topping:
2 eggs
100ml double cream
100ml crème fraîche
60g mozzarella cheese, grated
grated nutmeg
1 tsp mustard
1 tsp lemon zest
2 tbsp basil, finely chopped
500g cherry tomatoes, halved

To garnish:
basil leaves

Almond tart

Preparation time: 25 min
 plus 1 h chilling
Cooking time: 1 h 5 min
Serves 4–6

For the pastry:
200g plain flour
a pinch of salt
100g butter
1–2 tbsp water

For the filling:
3 eggs
150g sugar
150ml double cream
2 tbsp lemon juice
1 tsp grated lemon zest
75g butter
150g ground almonds

To decorate:
icing sugar

1. For the pastry, sift the flour into a mixing bowl and stir in the salt. Rub in the butter until the mixture resembles breadcrumbs. Gradually add the water, a tablespoon at a time, mixing continuously until the mixture just comes together as a dough. Roll the pastry into a ball, then wrap in cling film and chill for 1 hour.

2. Preheat the oven to 400°F (200°C). Grease a 23cm flan tin or dish.

3. Roll out the pastry on a floured work surface and line the dish. Prick the base of the pastry case several times with a fork. Cover the pastry with a sheet of non-stick baking paper and fill it with rice or dried beans. Bake for 20 minutes, until the pastry is pale golden. Remove from the oven and remove the beans and paper.

4. Reduce the oven temperature to 350°F (180°C).

5. For the filling, whisk the eggs and sugar with an electric whisk until fluffy. Whisk in the cream, lemon juice and zest then whisk in the butter.

6. Place the bowl over a pan of simmering (not boiling) water and whisk until creamy. Stir in the almonds.

7. Put the filling into the pastry case and bake for about 45 minutes, until the filling is firm and golden. Cool in the tin. Remove from the tin and sift over the icing sugar.

Pork pies

1. For the pastry, put the flour into a mixing bowl and stir in the butter, salt, egg and water. Mix with your hands to form a dough. Wrap in cling film and chill for 2 hours.

2. For the filling, mix all the ingredients together until well combined.

3. Preheat the oven to 350°F (180°C). Grease 12 deep muffin tins.

4. Roll out two-thirds of the pastry on a lightly floured surface and cut 12 pieces to fit the tins. Spoon in the meat mixture.

5. Roll out the remaining pastry and cut out 12 circles for the top of the pies. Brush with beaten egg yolk and place on top of the filling, sealing well. Brush the pies with the remaining beaten egg and pierce a hole in the centre of each pie.

6. Bake for 35–45 minutes until the pastry is golden and the filling is cooked. Cool in the tins.

Preparation time: 25 min
  plus 2 h chilling
Cooking time: 45 min
Serves 12

For the pastry:
400g plain flour
200g butter, melted
½ tsp salt
1 egg, beaten
2 tbsp water

For the filling:
1 slice bread, soaked in warm water
400g minced pork
60g minced fatty bacon
60g minced smoked bacon
2 shallots, chopped
2 garlic cloves, finely chopped
1 egg
1 tsp ground allspice

To finish:
1 egg yolk, for brushing

Rabbit pie with polenta crust

1. For the pastry, sift the flour into a mixing bowl and stir in the polenta and salt. Rub in the butter and lard until the mixture resembles breadcrumbs. Gradually add the water until the mixture just comes together as a dough. Roll the pastry into a ball, then wrap in cling film and chill for 1 hour.

2. For the filling, heat the oil in a pan and brown the meat in batches. Remove from the pan and set aside. Add the onions and garlic to the pan and season with salt and pepper. Stir in the flour and cook for 1 minute. Return the meat to the pan with the bay leaf. Cover and simmer for 30 minutes. Add the potatoes and carrots to the pan and continue cooking for 20 minutes. Remove from the heat and stir in the parsley.

3. Heat the oven to 400°F (200°C). Grease a large flan tin or pie dish.

4. Roll out two-thirds of the pastry on a floured work surface, until it is almost twice as wide as the diameter of the pie tin. Line the base and sides of the tin. Gently press the pastry into the corners of the tin, trimming off any excess. Put the filling into the pastry case.

5. Roll out the remaining pastry on a floured surface until it is slightly larger than the diameter of the pie tin. Place the pastry lid on top of the pie. Trim off any excess pastry. Seal the pastry lid to the pastry case by crimping the edges of the pastry lid with a fork. Bake for 35–45 minutes until the pastry is golden and the filling is piping hot.

Preparation time: 25 min
plus 1 h chilling
Cooking time: 1 h 35 min
Serves 4

For the pastry:
220g plain flour
100g polenta
1 tsp salt
90g butter
70g lard
2–3 tbsp water

For the filling:
3 tbsp oil
600g boneless rabbit meat, cubed
2 onions, chopped
2 garlic cloves, finely chopped
2 tbsp flour
1 bay leaf
500g potatoes, peeled and diced
400g carrots, diced
2 tbsp chopped parsley

Cheese and chard pie

1. For the pastry, sift the flour into a mixing bowl and stir in the salt. Rub in the butter until the mixture resembles breadcrumbs. Gradually add the egg yolk and water, a tablespoon at a time, mixing continuously until the mixture just comes together as a dough. (You may not need to use all the water). Roll the pastry into a ball, then wrap in cling film and chill for 1 hour.

2. Preheat the oven to 350°F (180°C). Line a 23cm loose-based tart tin. Roll out two-thirds of the pastry on a floured surface, until it is almost twice as wide as the diameter of the pie tin. Line the base and sides of the tin. Gently press the pastry into the corners of the tin, trimming off any excess, then prick the base of the pastry case several times with a fork. Cover the pastry with a sheet of non-stick baking paper and fill it with rice or dried beans. Bake for 10–15 minutes, until the pastry is pale golden. Remove from the oven, discard the beans and paper and set aside to cool.

3. For the filling, heat the oil in a pan and cook the onions until completely softened. Add the Swiss chard stalks and cook for 3 minutes, then add the leaves and cook until tender. Season and leave to cool.

4. Roll out the remaining pastry to a circle large enough to cover the pie. Mix together the eggs, cream and cheeses and season well. Spread the chard and onion over the base of the tart and pour the egg mix over.

5. Cover with the pastry lid and cut 2 slits in the top. Bake for 20–30 minutes, until the pastry is browned and the filling is just set.

Preparation time: 30 min
 plus 1 h chilling
Cooking time: 50 min
Serves 4

For the pastry:
450g plain flour
½ tsp salt
120g butter
1 egg yolk
120ml water

For the filling:
1 tbsp oil
2 onions, chopped
250g Swiss chard, leaves and stalks
 separated
4 eggs
142ml double cream
75g grated Gruyère cheese
2 tbsp grated Parmesan cheese

Beef and beer pie

1. For the pastry, sift the flour into a mixing bowl and stir in the salt. Rub in the butter until the mixture resembles breadcrumbs. Gradually add the water, a tablespoon at a time, mixing continuously until the mixture just comes together as a dough. (You may not need to use all of the water.) Roll the pastry into a ball, then wrap in cling film and chill for 1 hour.

2. For the filling, season the flour with a sprinkling of salt and pepper. Toss the meat in the seasoned flour to coat.

3. Heat 2 tablespoons oil in a large pan and brown the diced steak in batches. Remove the meat from the pan and set aside.

4. Add the remaining oil to the pan and cook the onions and mushrooms until lightly browned. Stir in the ale, Worcestershire sauce and stock, then add the meat. Bring to a simmer. Cover and cook on a low heat for 1–1 ½ hours until the meat is tender. Transfer to a pie dish and leave to cool.

5. Preheat the oven to 350°F (180°C).

6. Roll out the pastry on a floured surface until it is slightly larger than the dish. Wet the rim of the dish and place the pastry lid on top of the pie. Trim off any excess pastry. Seal the edges by pressing down well.

7. Bake for 30–40 minutes, until the pastry is light golden and the filling is piping hot.

Preparation time: 30 min
 plus 1 h chilling
Cooking time: 2 h 15 min
Serves 4

For the pastry:
225g plain flour
½ tsp salt
110g butter
2–3 tbsp water

For the filling:
1 tbsp plain flour
1kg braising steak, diced
3 tbsp oil
2 onions, chopped
110g mushrooms, quartered
220ml dark ale
1 tbsp Worcestershire sauce
200ml beef stock

Savoury tart with ricotta, peas and salmon

1. Preheat the oven to 375°F (180°C). Grease 4 ovenproof tart dishes about 15cm in diameter.

2. Roll out the pastry on a floured surface and cut 4 circles to fit the dishes. Line with the pastry circles.

3. Whisk the milk with the eggs and grated cheese and season well with salt and pepper. Pour the mixture into the tart cases and scatter over the salmon, peas and ricotta. Bake in the oven for 20–25 minutes until the filling is set. Garnish with the chives.

Preparation time: 25 min
Cooking time: 25 min
Serves 4

400g puff pastry
200ml milk
4 eggs
75g Emmental cheese, grated
200g salmon fillet, cut into strips
150g frozen peas
250g ricotta, crumbled
chopped chives, to serve

Filo pastry with spinach and feta cheese

Preparation time: 25 min
Cooking time: 45 min
Serves 4

500g spinach, stalks removed and
   leaves washed
2 tbsp vegetable oil
1 onion, finely chopped
1 garlic clove, finely chopped
a pinch of nutmeg
75g butter, melted
250g filo pastry sheets, defrosted
   if frozen
150g feta cheese, crumbled

1. Preheat the oven to 400°F (200°C).

2. Wilt the washed spinach in a large pan over a high heat, drain well, squeeze out any excess liquid and chop roughly.

3. Heat the oil in a pan and gently cook the onion until soft but not browned. Add the garlic, cook for 2 more minutes then mix into the spinach. Season with salt, pepper and the nutmeg and set aside.

4. Brush an ovenproof dish about 20cm x 15cm with a little of the melted butter and line the base with 3 sheets of the pastry, brushing each one with butter as you do so.

5. Spread the spinach mixture onto the pastry, scatter over the crumbled feta and top with the remaining pastry sheets, brushing each one with melted butter. Cut the pie into 4 portions then bake in the oven for 25–35 minutes or until the pastry is crisp and golden.

Vegetable tarts

1. For the pastry, sift the flour into a mixing bowl and stir in the salt. Rub in the butter until the mixture resembles breadcrumbs. Gradually add the egg and water, a tablespoon at a time, mixing continuously until the mixture just comes together as a dough. (You may not need to use all the water.) Roll the pastry into a ball, then wrap in cling film and chill for 30 minutes.

2. Heat the oven to 400°F (200°C). Grease 6 tart tins, 10cm in diameter.

3. Roll out the pastry on floured surface and line the tins. Prick the base of the pastry case several times with a fork.

4. Cover the pastry with a sheet of non-stick baking paper and fill it with rice or dried beans. Bake for 10–15 minutes, until the pastry is pale golden. Remove from the oven, discard the beans and paper and set aside to cool.

5. For the filling, blanch the mangetout, beans and carrots in boiling salted water for 3–4 minutes. Heat the oil and fry the peppers, tomatoes and courgettes until tender. Season well.

6. Pile the vegetables in to the pastry cases.

Preparation time: 25 min
 plus 30 min chilling
Cooking time: 25 min
Serves 6

For the pastry:
200g plain flour
½ tsp salt
100g butter
1 egg, beaten
2 tbsp water

For the filling:
600g mixed vegetables, (e.g. green beans, mangetout, yellow peppers, tomatoes, carrots, courgettes
oil, for frying

Cheese and ham pies

1. For the pastry, place the flour, salt and butter into a mixing bowl. Rub the butter into the flour until the mixture resembles breadcrumbs. Add the water and stir until the dough binds together. Wrap the pastry in cling film and chill for 30 minutes.

2. Heat the oven to 400°F (200°C). Grease 12 deep pie or muffin tins.

3. Roll out the pastry on a lightly floured surface and cut 12 rounds to fit the tins and 12 smaller rounds for the lids. Cut out a lattice pattern with a sharp knife or lattice cutter in the smaller rounds. Press the larger rounds into the tins.

4. For the filling, whisk the eggs with the cream and ricotta. Spread over the base of the pies. Sprinkle the ham over the top, then add the mozzarella and a sprinkling of peppercorns.

5. Brush the edges of each pie with a little egg and then place a lid on top, pressing the edges together to seal. Make a hole in the top of each pie, brush the tops with egg and bake for 20–25 minutes until the pastry is golden brown and the filling is piping hot.

Preparation time: 25 min
   plus 30 min chilling
Cooking time: 25 min
Serves 12

For the pastry:
300g plain flour
a pinch of salt
175g butter
3–4 tbsp water

For the filling:
3 eggs
400g ricotta cheese
240g cooked ham, chopped
300g grated mozzarella
1 tbsp peppercorns, lightly crushed

To finish:
1 egg, beaten

Spinach and sheep's cheese tart

1. For the pastry, sift the flour into a mixing bowl and stir in the salt. Rub in the butter until the mixture resembles breadcrumbs. Gradually add the egg, mixing continuously until the mixture just comes together as a dough. You may need to add a little water. Roll the pastry into a ball, then wrap in cling film and chill for 30 minutes.

2. Heat the oven to 350°F (180°C). Grease a 28cm flan or tart tin.

3. Roll out the pastry on a floured surface and line the tin. Prick the base several times with a fork and bake for 10 minutes.

4. For the filling, wash the spinach and put into a pan with the water just clinging to the leaves. Cook for a few minutes until just wilted. Drain the spinach, squeeze out the water and mix with the onion. Spread the mixture on the base of the pastry case.

5. Crumble the cheese and whisk with the yoghurt and eggs. Season with salt and pepper. Pour the mixture over the spinach and bake for 30 minutes until the filling is set. Allow to cool in the tin.

6. Place on a serving plate and garnish with rocket leaves.

Preparation time: 25 min
    plus 30 min chilling
Cooking time: 50 min
Serves 4–6

For the pastry:
200g plain flour
a pinch of salt
100g butter
1 egg, beaten

For the filling:
500g spinach
1 onion, chopped
1 tsp vegetable oil
250g feta
50ml plain yoghurt
2 eggs

To garnish:
rocket leaves

Apple tart

Preparation time: 25 min
  plus 30 min chilling
Cooking time: 50 min
Serves 4–6

For the pastry:
250g plain flour
1 tsp sugar
a pinch of salt
125g butter
1 egg yolk, beaten

For the filling:
1 packet custard powder
200ml dry white wine
150ml apple juice
4 tbsp sugar
800g apples, peeled and cored
1 egg white
3 tbsp apple jelly

1. For the pastry, sift the flour into a mixing bowl and stir in the sugar and salt. Rub in the butter until the mixture resembles breadcrumbs. Add the egg yolk, mixing continuously until the mixture just comes together as a dough. If it is too stiff, add a little water. Roll the pastry into a ball, then wrap in cling film and chill for 30 minutes.

2. Heat the oven to 350°F (180°C). Grease a 23cm deep flan tin.

3. Roll out the pastry on a floured surface and line the tin. Prick the pastry all over with a fork, line the pastry case with non-stick baking paper and fill it with rice or dried beans. Bake for 10 minutes. Remove the paper and beans.

4. For the filling, make the custard according to the directions on the packet, using the wine and apple juice instead of milk and the sugar.

5. Chop two-thirds of the apples and thinly slice the rest. Mix the chopped apples with the apple custard.

6. Whisk the egg white until stiff and fold into the apple custard. Spoon into the pastry case.

7. Arrange the sliced apples on top of the filling and bake for 40 minutes until the apples are beginning to brown and the filling is set. Brush the apples with the apple jelly while the tart is still warm. Leave to cool.

Banana tart with honey

1. Line a baking sheet with non-stick baking paper.

2. Roll out the pastry to a 23 x 35cm rectangle. Cut a 2.5cm-wide strip of pastry from each side. Place the rectangle on the baking sheet.

3. Mix together the egg yolk and water, and brush over the pastry. Place the strips on each side to form a border, pressing on firmly. Brush the strips with the egg. Chill for 20 minutes.

4. Heat the oven to 375°F (190°C).

5. Prick the bottom of the pastry all over with a fork. Bake for 30–40 minutes, until the shell is puffy and golden.

6. Increase the oven temperature to 425°F (220°C).

7. Rub the bananas with the lemon juice. Heat the sugar in a frying pan, stirring until melted. Cook without stirring until amber.

8. Remove from the heat and stir in the butter, vanilla and water. Add the bananas and gently turn to coat with the caramel.

9. Arrange the bananas in the pastry case, cut sides up, leaving most of the caramel in the pan. Stir the honey into the caramel and spoon over the bananas.

10. Bake for about 20 minutes, until the bananas are slightly tender.

Preparation time: 25 min
 plus 20 min chilling
Cooking time: 1 h
Serves 4

400g puff pastry
1 egg yolk
1½ tbsp water
3–4 firm bananas, halved
 lengthwise
1 ½ tbsp lemon juice
110g sugar
6 tbsp unsalted butter
½ tsp vanilla extract
2 tbsp water
2 tbsp honey

Meat pie with pistachios

1. Put the pork, garlic, thyme and brandy in a bowl, cover and leave to marinate for at least 2 hours.

2. Loosen the sausage meat with a fork, add it to the bowl with the marinated pork and mix well. Stir in the chives and pistachios and season well.

3. Preheat the oven to 350°F (180°C). Butter a 1kg terrine mould or loaf tin.

4. Roll out the pastry to a rectangle larger than the tin. Use two-thirds of the pastry to line the tin, letting it hang over the edge.

5. Place half the pork mixture in the tin and cover with the bacon slices. Cover with the remaining pork mixture.

6. Brush the pastry edges with whisked egg and bring up sides to meet down the centre of the filling. Place the remaining pastry on top and press to seal. Brush with beaten egg and bake for 45–50 minutes until the pastry is deep golden brown and the filling is cooked. Cover with foil if the pastry is browning too quickly.

Preparation time: 30 min
  plus 2 h marinating
Cooking time: 50 min
Serves 4–6

300g minced pork
2 garlic cloves, crushed
1 sprig thyme
2 tbsp brandy
1kg sausage meat
1 small bunch chives, chopped
110g pistachios
250g lean cooked bacon, sliced
500g shortcrust pastry
1 egg, beaten

Making
rich pastry

Preparing perfect pastry is not difficult, but it does require a little patience and attention to detail. An important factor in getting a melt-in-the-mouth texture is to allow the pastry to rest before rolling, so make sure you incorporate enough time for this step.

STEP 1 Sift the flour and salt onto a clean worksurface and scatter over the pieces of butter. Rub together until the mixture resembles fine breadcrumbs.

STEP 2 Once all the butter has been worked in, add in the sugar, a little at a time, evenly mixing it into the flour and butter mixture.

STEP 3 Make a well in the centre of the dry ingredients and break the eggs into it. Using fingertips, mix everything together to make a soft dough.

STEP 4 Gently shape the dough into a ball, being careful not to overwork it with your hands. Wrap in cling film and chill for at least 4 hours.

STEP 5 Remove the now-firm pastry from the fridge and place it on a floured work surface. Roll it out to fit your flan tray.

Feta and pea tart

1. For the pastry, put the flour in a heap on a work surface, mix with the salt and make a well in the middle of the flour. Cut the butter into small pieces and scatter around the well. Break the egg into the middle and chop all the ingredients with a knife until they have the consistency of breadcrumbs. Quickly knead to a dough by hand, form into a ball, wrap in cling film and chill for about 30 minutes.

2. Heat the oven to 400°F (200°C). Grease a 23cm springform flan tin.

3. For the filling, mix together the cheese, onion, peas, chives and garlic.

4. Whisk the eggs and stir in the cream. Season with salt and pepper.

5. Roll out the pastry on a floured surface and line the tin.

6. Spread the pea mixture on the pastry, pour the egg and cream mixture over and bake for about 35 minutes until the filling is set. Sprinkle with ground pepper. Serve warm.

Preparation time: 25 min
  plus 30 min chilling
Cooking time: 35 min
Serves 4

For the pastry:
250g plain flour
a pinch of salt
125g butter
1 egg

For the filling:
250g feta cheese, crumbled
1 onion, chopped
250g peas, frozen
1 bunch chives, chopped
3 garlic cloves, finely chopped
4 eggs
200ml double cream

Mushroom and bacon tart

1. For the pastry, sift the flour into a mixing bowl and stir in the salt. Rub in the butter until the mixture resembles breadcrumbs. Gradually add the water, a tablespoon at a time, mixing continuously until the mixture just comes together as a dough. (You may not need to use all of the water.) Roll the pastry into a ball, then wrap in cling film and chill for 1 hour.

2. Heat the oven to 350°F (180°C). Grease a 25cm flan tin.

3. For the filling, heat the oil in a pan and cook the shallots until translucent. Add the bacon and mushrooms and cook until just browned. Stir in the sherry vinegar, soy sauce, salt and pepper.

4. Mix together the crème fraîche, cream, parsley and grated cheese.

5. Roll out the pastry on a floured surface and line the tin.

6. Spread the mushroom mixture on base of the pastry case. Pour over the cream mixture and bake for about 35 minutes until the filling is set and the pastry is golden.

Preparation time: 25 min
  plus 1 h chilling
Cooking time: 45 min
Serves 4–6

For the pastry:
225g plain flour
½ tsp salt
110g butter
2–3 tbsp water

For the filling:
3 tbsp oil
4 shallots, chopped
125g bacon, cut into strips
750g oyster mushrooms, sliced
1 tsp sherry vinegar
1 tbsp light soy sauce
150ml crème fraîche
100ml double cream
1 tbsp chopped parsley
100g grated Gruyère cheese

Passion fruit tartlet

1. For the pastry, sift the flour into a mixing bowl and rub in the butter until the mixture resembles breadcrumbs. Stir in the sugar and beat in the egg yolks. Gradually add the water, a tablespoon at a time, mixing continuously until the mixture just comes together as a dough. (You may not need to use all of the water.) Roll the pastry into a ball, then wrap in cling film and chill for 1 hour.

2. Preheat the oven to 350°F (180°C). Grease 4 x 10cm loose-based deep tart tins.

3. Roll out the pastry on a floured surface and line the tins. Prick the pastry all over with a fork, line the pastry cases with non-stick baking paper and fill with rice or dried beans. Bake for 15 minutes. Remove the paper and beans and bake for a further 5 minutes.

4. For the filling, put the sugar, fruit purée and butter into a pan and bring to a boil, stirring. Remove from the heat and cool slightly. Beat in the egg yolks. Return to the heat and stir over a low heat for about 4 minutes, until slightly thickened. Do not boil.

5. Spoon the filling into the pastry cases and bake for 10 minutes until the filling is set. Leave to cool before removing from the tins.

6. Scatter the passion fruit seeds over the top.

Preparation time: 25 min
  plus 1 h chilling
Cooking time: 35 min
Serves 4

For the pastry:
225g plain flour
110g butter
50g caster sugar
2 egg yolks
2–3 tbsp water

For the filling:
110g sugar
250ml fresh or frozen passion fruit
  purée
75g unsalted butter
3 egg yolks, beaten

To decorate:
seeds from 2 passion fruit

Nettle tart

Preparation time: 25 min
 plus 1 h chilling
Cooking time: 40 min
Serves 4–6

For the pastry:
60g plain flour
100g wholemeal spelt flour
a pinch of salt
80g butter
2 tbsp water
sesame seeds

For the filling:
2 handfuls nettle leaves
400g ricotta cheese
2 eggs
1 egg yolk
50–70g grated Gouda cheese

1. Preheat the oven to 400°F (200°C). Butter a 20cm springform pan or tart tin and sprinkle with sesame seeds.

2. For the pastry, sift the flour into a mixing bowl and stir in the salt. Rub in the butter until the mixture resembles breadcrumbs. Gradually add the water, a tablespoon at a time, mixing continuously until the mixture just comes together as a dough. (You may not need to use all of the water.) Roll the pastry into a ball, then wrap in cling film and chill for 1 hour.

3. For the filling, reserve a few nettle leaves for the garnish. Wash the remaining nettles, shake dry and blanch briefly in boiling, salted water. Drain, refresh in cold water, drain thoroughly, then chop roughly.

4. Whisk the ricotta with the eggs and egg yolk and season with salt and pepper. Stir in the chopped nettles.

5. Roll out the pastry and line the tin. Spread the egg mixture in the tin and sprinkle with cheese. Bake for about 35 minutes until the filling is set.

6. Serve scattered with nettle leaves.

Chicken and leek pot pies

1. For the pastry, sift the flour into a mixing bowl and stir in the salt. Rub in the butter until the mixture resembles breadcrumbs. Gradually add water until the mixture just comes together as a dough. Roll the pastry into a ball, then wrap in cling film and chill for 30 minutes.

2. Preheat the oven to 400°F (200°C). Grease 4 individual deep pie dishes.

3. Toss the chicken in the cornflour.

4. Heat the oil in a pan, add the leeks, then fry for 3 minutes until starting to soften. Add the chicken and water then bring to the boil, stirring. Reduce the heat and simmer for 10 minutes, until the chicken is just tender. Remove from the heat, then stir in the cream and mustard.

5. Spoon the chicken filling into the pie dishes.

6. Roll out the dough on a lightly floured surface and cut out 4 circles, slightly larger than the diameter of the dishes. Place the pastry lids on top of the pies and seal well.

7. Make 2 small holes in the centre of the pastry lids. Brush with beaten egg.

8. Bake for about 25 minutes until the pastry is crisp and golden.

Preparation time: 20 min
  plus 30 min chilling
Cooking time: 45 min
Serves 4

For the pastry:
225g flour
110g butter
a pinch of salt

For the filling:
500g boneless skinless chicken
  breasts, roughly chopped
2 tsp cornflour
1 tbsp oil
4 leeks, sliced
200ml water
2 tbsp double cream
1 tbsp wholegrain mustard

To finish:
1 egg, beaten

Fig tart

1. Beat together the butter and sugar until smooth. Mix in the egg. Sift in the flour, salt, and baking powder and stir until the mixture just comes together. Shape into a ball, wrap in cling film and chill for 30 minutes.

2. Preheat the oven to 350°F (180°C). Lightly butter a 23cm loose-based flan tin.

3. Press the pastry into the bottom and sides of the tin.

4. Spread the jam evenly over the base of the pastry case and bake for 20–25 minutes, until the pastry is golden brown. Cool in the tin, then place on a serving plate.

5. Place the figs over the jam filling in concentric circles. Sift a little icing sugar over the pastry edges.

Preparation time: 20 min
  plus 30 min chilling
Cooking time: 25 min
Serves 4–6

6 tbsp butter
80g sugar
1 large egg
175g plain flour
a pinch of salt
1 tsp baking powder
450g fig jam
6–8 fresh figs, sliced
icing sugar

Egg and bacon pie

1. Preheat the oven to 400°F (200°C). Grease a 25cm pie tin.

2. Roll out the pastry slightly bigger than the tin. Line the tin with the pastry. Cut out a few decorative shapes from the pastry trimmings. Brush the edge of the pastry with water and decorate with the cut-out shapes, pressing on lightly.

3. Mix the sour cream with the parsley, seasonings and diced bacon and put into the pastry case. Carefully break the eggs on top.

4. Bake for about 20 minutes, until the eggs are set. Sprinkle with the parsley and serve immediately.

Preparation time: 25 min
Cooking time: 20 min
Serves 4

300g puff pastry
200ml sour cream
3 tbsp chopped parsley
1 pinch paprika
125g diced cooked bacon
4 eggs

To garnish:
2 tbsp chopped parsley

Blackberry and apricot tart with jelly

Preparation time: 25 min
  plus 1 h chilling
Cooking time: 20 min
Serves 4–6

For the pastry:
225g plain flour
2 tbsp icing sugar
110g butter
2–3 tbsp water

For the filling:
14 apricots, skinned, pitted and
  halved
75g sugar
2 tbsp water
1 packet lemon jelly
110g blackberries

1. For the pastry, sift the flour and icing sugar into a mixing bowl. Rub in the butter until the mixture resembles breadcrumbs. Gradually add the water, a tablespoon at a time, mixing continuously until the mixture just comes together as a dough. (You may not need to use all of the water.) Roll the pastry into a ball, then wrap in cling film and chill for 1 hour.

2. Preheat the oven to 375°F (190°C). Grease a 23cm flan or tart tin.

3. Roll out the pastry on a floured surface and line the tin. Prick the pastry all over with a fork, line the pastry case with non-stick baking paper and fill it with rice or dried beans. Bake for 20 minutes until golden and cooked. Remove the paper and beans and leave to cool.

4. For the filling, put 12 apricot halves in a pan with the sugar and water. Bring to the boil and simmer until the apricots are soft. Sieve the mixture into a bowl and leave to cool.

5. Spoon the apricot purée onto the base of the pastry case. Arrange the remaining apricot halves on top. Make the jelly according to the packet instructions and leave to cool, but not set. Spoon the jelly over the apricots and chill until set.

6. Decorate with the blackberries.

Ricotta and leek tart

1. Roll out the pastry and cut out 4 squares. Make a shallow cut all the way around the squares 1 cm in from the edge.

2. Preheat the oven to 400°F (200°C). Grease a large baking sheet.

3. Heat the oil and cook the leeks until soft, but not browned. Stir in the thyme and leave to cool.

4. Beat the ricotta with the eggs, then stir in the leeks and mix well. Season with salt and pepper.

5. Put the pastry squares on the baking tray. Spoon the leek mixture in the centre of the pastry, leaving the cut edge clear.

6. Bake for about 20 minutes until the pastry is golden brown. Serve warm garnished with thyme and salad leaves.

Preparation time: 20 min
Cooking time: 30 min
Serves 4

450g puff pastry
2 tbsp olive oil
4 leeks, sliced
1 tbsp chopped thyme
225g ricotta cheese
2 large eggs, beaten
thyme and salad leaves, to serve

South African milk tart with mandarin liqueur

1. For the pastry, sift the flour into a mixing bowl and stir in the salt. Rub in the butter until the mixture resembles breadcrumbs. Gradually add the water, a tablespoon at a time, mixing continuously until the mixture just comes together as a dough. (You may not need to use all of the water.) Roll the pastry into a ball, then wrap in cling film and chill for 1 hour.

2. Preheat the oven to 400°F (200°C). Grease 6 deep 10cm tart tins.

3. Roll out the pastry and line the tins. Then line each one with non-stick baking paper and baking beans, and bake for 10–15 minutes until the pastry is crisp and golden. Remove the paper and beans and bake for 4–5 minutes to dry the base of the pastry. Cool in the tins, then place on a wire rack to cool completely.

4. For the filling, heat the milk in a pan. Whisk in the flour, cornflour, butter, vanilla and 2 teaspoons cinnamon. Bring to a boil, stirring constantly, until the mixture thickens. Cool slightly.

5. Beat in the egg yolks, mixing thoroughly. Stir in the liqueur.

6. Whisk the egg whites until stiff peaks form. Fold in the sugar until incorporated. Fold the egg yolk mixture into the whisked egg whites.

7. Spoon the mixture into the pastry cases and leave to cool. Sprinkle with cinnamon and chill until set.

Preparation time: 25 min
 plus 1 h chilling
Cooking time: 20 min
Serves 6

For the pastry:
500g plain flour
1 tsp salt
220g butter
4–5 tbsp water

For the filling:
600ml milk
4 tbsp plain flour
2 tsp cornflour
2 tbsp butter
2 tsp vanilla extract
6 tsp ground cinnamon
4 eggs, separated
2–3 tbsp mandarin liqueur
4 tsp sugar

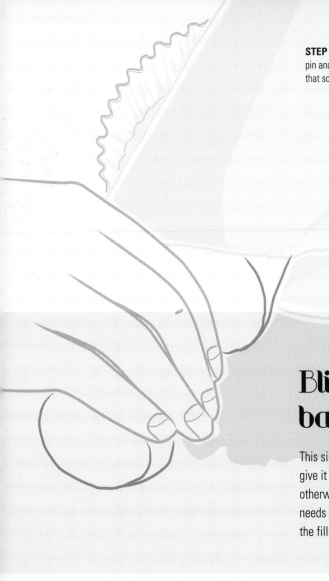

STEP 1 Fold the rolled-out pastry over the rolling pin and carefully lift it on top of the flan tin, so that some pastry overhangs each side.

Blind baking

This simple technique involves baking a pastry case to give it a crisp texture before you add the filling, which otherwise would make the pastry soggy. The pastry needs partial or full baking, depending on how moist the filling is that is being used.

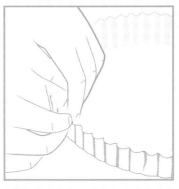

STEP 2 Using your fingertips, gently press the pastry into the bottom of the tray then up the sides, taking care not to tear it. Trim away excess pastry.

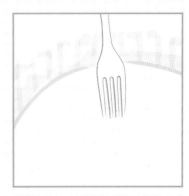

STEP 3 Using a fork, prick all over the base of the pastry gently and evenly. Once done, cover with cling film and refrigerate the pastry for 30 minutes.

STEP 4 Cut a piece of baking parchment large enough to cover the base and side of the pastry. Position in place and cover with baking beans.

STEP 5 Bake at 350°F (180°C) for 18–20 minutes to partially bake. To fully bake, remove the parchment and bake for 6–7 minutes. Trim any excess pastry.

Raspberry tart

1. For the pastry, sift the flour into a mixing bowl and stir in the almonds. Rub in the butter until the mixture resembles breadcrumbs. Stir in the sugar. Gradually add the egg yolk and just enough water until the mixture just comes together as a dough. Wrap in cling film and chill for 1 hour.

2. Preheat the oven to 375°F (190°C). Line a large baking tray with non-stick baking paper.

3. Pat the pastry out into a circle on the baking tray, raising the edges to form a border. Line the tart case with non-stick baking paper and baking beans, and bake for 20 minutes until the edges are starting to brown. Remove the beans and paper, then continue to cook for 10 minutes until cooked. Leave to cool. Reduce the oven temperature to 300°F (170°C).

4. For the filling, whisk the crème fraîche with the eggs, sugar, vanilla, lemon juice and zest until thick. Spread over the bottom of the tart case. Place a quarter of the raspberries on top and bake for 15–20 minutes until the filling is set. Leave to cool.

5. Place the remaining raspberries on top and sift over a little icing sugar.

Preparation time: 25 min
 plus 1 h chilling
Cooking time: 50 min
Serves 4

For the pastry:
225g plain flour
175g ground almonds
225g cold butter, diced
175g caster sugar
1 egg yolk, beaten

For the filling:
200ml crème fraîche
2 eggs
75g caster sugar
½ tsp vanilla essence
1 lemon, juice and zest
500g raspberries
icing sugar

Aubergine, tomato and mozzarella tarts

1. Preheat the oven to 400°F (200°C). Line a baking tray with non-stick baking paper.

2. Finely chop the tomatoes, adding a little of the tomato oil, until it resembles a paste.

3. Roll out the puff pastry and cut out 12 circles 8cm in diameter, using a cookie cutter. Spoon some of the tomato paste on the top and season with pepper. Place a slice of mozzarella on top of the tomato paste, followed by some slices of aubergine.

4. Sprinkle with a few pine nuts, drizzle olive oil over the top and place on the baking tray. Bake for 15–20 minutes.

5. Garnish with a few rocket leaves and serve.

Preparation time: 20 min
Cooking time: 20 min
Serves 12

400g puff pastry
200g sundried tomatoes, in oil
3 balls mozzarella, thinly sliced
1 aubergine, sliced
4 tbsp pine nuts, toasted
olive oil
24 rocket leaves, stalks removed,
  to serve

Pea quiche

1. For the pastry, sift the flour into a mixing bowl and stir in the salt. Rub in the butter until the mixture resembles breadcrumbs. Gradually add the egg and water, a tablespoon at a time, mixing continuously until the mixture just comes together as a dough. (You may not need to use all of the water.) Roll the pastry into a ball, then wrap in cling film and chill for 30 minutes.

2. For the filling, heat the butter in a pan and cook the onion until soft. Add the lettuce and sprinkle in the flour. Pour in the stock and bring to a boil.

3. Add the peas and parsley and simmer gently for 15 minutes. Leave to cool slightly, then purée in a blender. Beat in the soured cream and eggs, and season with salt and pepper.

4. Heat the oven to 350°F (180°C). Grease a 26cm flan or tart tin.

5. Roll out the pastry on a floured surface and line the tin.

6. Prick the base of the pastry case several times with a fork. Cover the pastry with a sheet of non-stick baking paper and fill it with rice or dried beans. Bake for 10 minutes, until the pastry is pale golden. Remove from the oven, discard the beans and paper and set aside to cool.

7. Spoon in the filling and bake for 30 minutes until the pastry is golden brown. Serve warm garnished with the bacon.

Preparation time: 25 min
  plus 30 min chilling
Cooking time: 45 min
Serves 4–6

For the pastry:
200g plain flour
1 tsp salt
100g butter
1 egg, beaten
4 tbsp water

For the filling:
40g butter
1 onion, chopped
1 lettuce heart, torn into pieces
1 tbsp flour
400ml chicken stock
500g peas, frozen
2 tbsp chopped parsley
250ml soured cream
3 eggs

To garnish:
6 slices cooked bacon

Courgette and feta tart with mint

Preparation time: 20 min
Cooking time: 20 min
Serves 4

1 tsp olive oil
3 courgettes, quartered length-
ways and cut into 4cm-thick
pieces
3 eggs
2 garlic cloves
250ml milk
200g crumbled feta cheese
2 tbsp chopped mint
1 tbsp chopped parsley
mint sprigs, to serve

1. Preheat the oven to 375°F (190°C).

2. Brush a 20cm round tin with the oil and lay the courgette pieces in it.

3. Put the eggs, garlic, milk, feta and mint and parsley in a blender and purée. Season with salt and ground black pepper and pour over the courgettes.

4. Bake for 20 minutes until golden brown.

5. Remove from the oven, place a plate over the top and upturn the frittata onto a dish. Serve garnished with mint.

Watercress tart

1. For the pastry, put all the ingredients into a mixing bowl and beat well to form a soft dough. Wrap in cling film and chill for 1 hour.

2. Preheat the oven to 350°F (180°C). Grease a 20cm pie tin or dish.

3. Roll out the pastry on a floured work surface, until it is almost twice as wide as the diameter of the pie tin. Line the base and sides of the tin. Gently press the pastry into the corners of the tin, trimming off any excess, then prick the base of the pastry case several times with a fork.

4. Cover the pastry with a sheet of non-stick baking paper and fill it with rice or dried beans. Bake for 15–20 minutes, until the pastry is pale golden. Remove from the oven, discard the beans and paper and set aside to cool.

5. For the filling, put the watercress, garlic, pine nuts and creme fraiche in a food processor and process until smooth. Stir in the eggs, cream and cheese and season with salt, pepper and nutmeg.

6. Pour into the pastry case and bake for 25 minutes until the filling is set. Cool in the tin. Sprinkle with toasted pine nuts.

Preparation time: 20 min
   plus 1 h chilling
Cooking time: 45 min
Serves 4

For the pastry:
150g plain flour
75g butter, softened
1 egg
½ tsp salt

For the filling:
75–100g watercress
2 garlic cloves
50g pine nuts, toasted
150ml creme fraiche
2 eggs
125ml double cream
4 tbsp grated Parmesan cheese
grated nutmeg

To garnish:
toasted pine nuts

Rhubarb tart

1. For the pastry, sift the flour into a mixing bowl and stir in the salt. Rub in the butter until the mixture resembles breadcrumbs. Stir in the sugar, then gradually add the egg, until the mixture just comes together. If it is too stiff add a little water. Roll the pastry into a ball, then wrap in cling film and chill for 30 minutes.

2. Heat the oven to 350°F (180°C). Grease a 25cm tart tin.

3. Roll out the pastry on a floured surface and line the tin. Prick the pastry all over with a fork, line the pastry cases with non-stick baking paper and fill with rice or dried beans. Bake for 15 minutes. Remove the paper and beans.

4. For the filling, toss the rhubarb with 100g sugar and the cinnamon.

5. Beat the crème fraîche with the remaining sugar, eggs and lemon juice.

6. Put the rhubarb on the base of the pastry case and pour over the egg mixture. Bake for about 30 minutes, until the filling is set and the pastry is golden.

Preparation time: 20 min
  plus 30 min chilling
Cooking time: 45 min
Serves 4–6

For the pastry:
300g plain flour
a pinch of salt
150g cold butter
70g sugar
1 egg, whisked

For the topping:
400g rhubarb, cut into 7cm pieces
200g sugar
1 tsp ground cinnamon
200ml crème fraîche
4 eggs
juice of 1 lemon

Small cherry lattice pie

1. For the pastry, put the flour in a mixing bowl and rub in the butter until the mixture resembles breadcrumbs. Add the caster sugar and egg yolks and mix to a dough. If it is too stiff add a little cold water. Wrap in cling film and chill for 20 minutes.

2. Preheat the oven to 375°F (190°C). Grease 4 small deep cake or pie tins.

3. Roll out two-thirds of the pastry on a floured surface and line the tins.

4. For the filling, mix together the cherries, sugar, Amaretto and marzipan. Put into the pastry cases.

5. Roll out the remaining pastry and cut out strips. Arrange the strips on top of the cherry filling, to form a lattice pattern. Brush with beaten egg.

6. Bake for 20–25 minutes until the pastry is crisp and golden. Cool in the tins.

7. Sift a little icing sugar over the cooled pies.

Preparation time: 20 min
plus 20 min chilling
Cooking time: 25 min
Serves 4

For the pastry:
400g plain flour
200g butter
50g caster sugar
2 egg yolks

For the filling:
500g cherries, pitted
3 tbsp sugar
1 tbsp Amaretto liqueur
100g marzipan, finely chopped

To finish:
1 egg, beaten
icing sugar

Sausage, apple and onion tart

Preparation time: 20 min
  plus 1 h chilling
Cooking time: 45 min
Serves 4

For the pastry:
225g plain flour
½ tsp salt
110g butter
2–3 tbsp water

For the filling:
2 tbsp oil
6 sausages
2 onions, chopped
1 cooking apple, peeled, cored
  and chopped
6 eggs
125ml milk

To serve:
plum and apple chutney

1. For the pastry. sift the flour into a mixing bowl and stir in the salt. Rub in the butter until the mixture resembles breadcrumbs. Gradually add the water, a tablespoon at a time, mixing continuously until the mixture just comes together as a dough. (You may not need to use all of the water.) Roll the pastry into a ball, then wrap in cling film and chill for 1 hour.

2. Heat the oven to 400°F (200°C). Butter a rectangular tart tin.

3. Roll out the pastry on a floured surface, to fit the tin. Line the base and sides of the tin. Gently press the pastry into the corners of the tin, trimming off any excess.

4. For the filling, heat the oil and brown the sausages on all sides. Remove from the pan, and add the onion and apple to the pan and cook until just soft, but not browned. Place the sausages, onions and apple on the base of the pastry case.

5. Whisk together the eggs and milk and season with salt and pepper. Pour over the sausages and bake for 25–30 minutes until the filling is set and the pastry is golden.

6. Serve hot or warm with the chutney.

Quince tarte tatin

1. Heat the butter and sugar in an ovenproof frying pan until melted, stirring occasionally.

2. Remove the pan from the heat and arrange the quinces in the pan, fitting them together tightly. Return the pan to the heat and bring to a boil.

3. Cook slowly for 20–40 minutes, depending on the ripeness of the fruit, until the mixture becomes caramel coloured. Remove from the heat and leave to cool.

4. Preheat the oven to 425°F (220°C).

5. Roll out the pastry 5 cm larger than the pan and place it carefully over the quinces, pressing the sides to the edges of the pan.

6. Bake for 20–25 minutes until the pastry is golden. Remove from the oven and leave to cool for 10 minutes. Run a knife around the edge of the pastry. Place a serving plate over the pan and invert onto the plate.

Preparation time: 20 min
Cooking time: 1 h 5 min
Serves 4

110g unsalted butter
200g caster sugar
4–6 ripe quinces, peeled and quartered
350g puff pastry

Pear tart

1. For the pastry, put the flour, ground walnuts, sugar and salt in a heap on a work surface and make a well in the centre. Cut the butter into small flakes and scatter around the well. Break the egg into the centre and quickly work all the ingredients to a pliable dough. Wrap in cling film and chill for 30 minutes.

2. Put the water into a pan with the honey, the seeds scraped out of the vanilla pod, the vanilla pod and the lemon juice. Bring to the boil and boil over a high heat for 3 minutes. Remove the vanilla pod.

3. Preheat the oven to 350°F (180°C). Grease a tart tin.

4. Roll out the pastry on a floured surface and line the tin.

5. Sprinkle 5 pears with lemon juice and 4 tablespoons of the honey syrup. Slice the remaining pears.

6. Line the sides and base of the pastry case with pear slices and stand the whole pears in the tin.

7. Mix the crème fraîche with the egg yolks and the remaining honey syrup.

8. Whisk the egg whites until they form stiff peaks, then stir in the icing sugar. Lightly fold the beaten egg white into the egg yolk mixture and spread over and around the sliced pears.

9. Bake for 40 minutes. About 10 minutes before the end of the baking time, dust generously with icing sugar and allow to caramelise.

Preparation time: 25 min
plus 30 min chilling
Cooking time: 50 min
Serves 4–6

For the pastry:
150g plain flour
100g finely ground walnuts
80g sugar
a pinch of salt
150g cold butter
1 egg

For the filling:
100ml water
2 tbsp honey
1 vanilla pod
2 tbsp lemon juice
1kg pears, peeled and cored
200ml crème fraîche
2 eggs, separated
30g icing sugar

To finish:
icing sugar

Salmon quiche

1. For the pastry, sift the flour into a mixing bowl and stir in the salt. Rub in the butter until the mixture resembles breadcrumbs. Gradually add the water, a tablespoon at a time, mixing continuously until the mixture just comes together as a dough. (You may not need to use all of the water.) Roll the pastry into a ball, then wrap in cling film and chill for 1 hour.

2. Preheat the oven to 350°F (180°C). Butter a square baking dish.

3. Roll out the pastry on a floured surface and line the dish, overhanging the sides of the dish. Prick the pastry all over with a fork, line the pastry case with non-stick baking paper and fill it with rice or dried beans. Bake for 20 minutes. Remove the paper and beans.

4. For the filling, place the smoked salmon and tomatoes evenly in the base of the pastry case.

5. Beat together the eggs, crème fraîche and nutmeg until well combined. Season to taste with salt and freshly ground black pepper. Pour the mixture into the pastry case. Sprinkle with chives.

6. Bake for about 30 minutes, until the filling is set and the pastry is golden.

Preparation time: 20 min
  plus 1 h chilling
Cooking time: 50 min
Serves 4

For the pastry:
225g plain flour
½ tsp salt
110g butter
2–3 tbsp water

For the filling:
175g smoked salmon, chopped
4 tomatoes, quartered
3 eggs
200ml crème fraîche
1 tsp grated nutmeg
2 tbsp snipped chives

Sardine tart

1. For the pastry, sift the flour into a mixing bowl and stir in the salt. Rub in the butter until the mixture resembles breadcrumbs. Gradually add the egg, until the mixture just comes together as a dough. It it is too dry add a little water. Roll the pastry into a ball, then wrap in cling film and chill for 1 hour.

2. Preheat the oven to 350°F (180°C). Grease a 23cm flan tin or dish.

3. Roll out the pastry on a floured surface and line the tin.

4. For the filling, heat the oil in a frying pan and cook the shallots until soft but not browned. Drain off the oil and stir in the lemon juice. Season with salt and pepper.

5. Beat together the cream and eggs and mix with the shallot mixture.

6. Arrange the sardines on the base of the pastry case and pour over the cream mixture.

7. Bake for 30 minutes until the filling is set and the pastry is golden. Garnish with lemon wedges.

Preparation time: 20 min
  plus 1 h chilling
Cooking time: 40 min
Serves 4–6

For the pastry:
300g plain flour
1 tsp salt
125g butter
1 egg, beaten

For the filling:
1 tbsp oil
2 shallots, chopped
3–4 tbsp lemon juice
250ml double cream
2 eggs
250–300g canned sardines, drained

To garnish:
lemon wedges

Spinach and Roquefort tart with walnuts

1. For the pastry, beat all the ingredients together in a mixing bowl to a smooth dough. Wrap in cling film and chill for 30 minutes.

2. For the filling, heat the oil in a pan and cook the onion until soft, but not browned. Add the spinach and cook until just wilted. Leave to cool.

3. Preheat the oven to 350°F (180°C). Grease a 23cm springform tart tin.

4. Roll out two-thirds of the dough on a floured work surface, until it is almost twice as wide as the diameter of the pie tin. Line the base and sides of the tin. Gently press the pastry into the corners of the tin, trimming off any excess, then prick the base of the pastry case several times with a fork.

5. Cover the pastry with a sheet of non-stick baking paper and fill it with rice or dried beans. Bake for 10 minutes, until the pastry is pale golden. Remove from the oven, discard the beans and paper and set aside to cool.

6. Spread the spinach mixture on the base of the pastry case.

7. Beat together the cheese, cream, yoghurt and eggs and season with salt and pepper. Pour over the spinach. Sprinkle with walnuts.

8. Bake for 30 minutes until the filling is set and the pastry is golden brown. Serve warm.

Preparation time: 20 min
plus 30 min chilling
Cooking time: 50 min
Serves 4–6

For the pastry:
200g plain flour
100g butter
1 egg, beaten
a pinch of salt

For the filling:
1 tbsp oil
1 onion, chopped
500g spinach
250g Roquefort cheese, crumbled
100ml cream
50ml yoghurt
2 eggs
100g chopped walnuts

Mozzarella, olive and tomato pie

Preparation time: 20 min
  plus 1 h chilling
Cooking time: 45 min
Serves 4

For the pastry:
450g plain flour
½ tsp salt
120g butter
1 egg yolk
120ml water

For the filling:
12 slices mozzarella cheese
4 large tomatoes, sliced
1 garlic clove, chopped
110g black olives, pitted and
  halved
olive oil

1. For the pastry, sift the flour into a mixing bowl and stir in the salt. Rub in the butter until the mixture resembles breadcrumbs. Gradually add the egg yolk and water, a tablespoon at a time, mixing continuously until the mixture just comes together as a dough. (You may not need to use all of the water.) Roll the dough into a ball, then wrap in cling film and chill for 1 hour. Preheat the oven to 350°F (180°C). Grease a 20cm pie tin or dish.

2. Roll out two-thirds of the pastry on a floured work surface, until it is almost twice as wide as the diameter of the pie tin. Line the base and sides of the tin. Gently press the pastry into the corners of the tin, trimming off any excess, then prick the base of the pastry case several times with a fork. Cover the pastry with a sheet of non-stick baking paper and fill it with rice or dried beans. Bake for 10–15 minutes, until the pastry is pale golden. Remove from the oven, discard the beans and paper, and set aside to cool.

3. Arrange the mozzarella and tomatoes on the base. Scatter over the garlic, some salt and ground black pepper and the olives. Drizzle with olive oil.

4. Roll out the remaining pastry until it's slightly larger than the pie tin. Brush the rim of the cooked pastry case with some of the beaten egg and place the lid on the pie. Trim off any excess. Seal the lid to the case by crimping the edges of the lid with a fork.

5. Make two small holes in the centre of the pastry lid. Brush with the remaining beaten egg and bake for 25–30 minutes until golden-brown.

Pepper and mushroom tart with filo pastry

1. Preheat the oven to 400°F (200°C). Brush a 23cm loose-based tart tin with some of the melted butter and lay a sheet of filo on top. Brush with more butter and top with another layer of filo. Continue, overlapping the sheets over the rim of the tin, until all the sheets of filo pastry have been used.

2. Bake for 5 minutes until just beginning to crisp.

3. For the filling, heat the butter and oil together in a large pan. Add the mushrooms and cook for 10 minutes.

4. Add the peppers, increase the heat and cook for 5–10 minutes until soft. Season and add the thyme.

5. Scatter the cheese on the base of the pastry case and spoon in the filling. Bake for about 10 minutes until the filling is piping hot.

6. Cool in the tin. Garnish with chives.

Preparation time: 20 min
Cooking time: 35 min
Serves 4

200g filo pastry
75g butter, melted

For the filling:
1 tbsp butter
1 tbsp olive oil
200g mushrooms, quartered
4 red peppers, cut into strips
2 tbsp chopped fresh thyme
250g brie, chopped

To garnish:
snipped chives

Potato and rosemary quiche with buffalo mozzarella and olives

1. For the base, mix the flour and salt together in a mixing bowl. Dissolve the yeast in the lukewarm water and gradually add to the flour. Mix well to a dough. Knead well for 5 minutes.

2. Shape the dough into a ball, cover with a tea towel and leave to rest for 5 minutes.

3. Knead the dough and form into a ball. Cover as before and leave to rise in a warm place for 30 minutes.

4. Boil the potato slices for 5–6 minutes until just tender. Drain and toss with 1 tablespoon olive oil and the garlic and rosemary.

5. Preheat the oven to 425°F (225°C). Grease a large baking tray.

6. Flatten the dough and roll out thinly. Place on the baking tray.

7. Cover with the potato slices. Scatter the mozzarella and Parmesan cheese over. Sprinkle over the olives and drizzle with the remaining oil.

8. Bake for 10–15 minutes until the base is crisp and the topping is piping hot.

Preparation time: 15 min
plus 30 min rising
Cooking time: 20 min
Serves 4

For the base:
250g strong plain bread flour
½ tsp salt
½ tsp fresh yeast
160ml lukewarm water

For the topping:
10 small unpeeled waxy potatoes,
thinly sliced
2 tbsp olive oil
1 garlic clove, crushed
1 tbsp chopped rosemary
200g buffalo mozzarella cheese,
sliced
110g black olives, pitted
100g grated Parmesan

Chicken and ham pie

1. For the pastry, mix the flour and salt in a bowl and make a well in the centre. Bring the water and lard to a boil in a pan, then stir it into the flour to form a smooth dough. Cover and leave for 15 minutes. Preheat oven to 400°F (200°C). Line a deep pie tin about 20cm x 5cm deep. Roll out two-thirds of the pastry into a circle that will line the tin and overlap the edge. Ease the pastry into the tin, pressing into the corners with it just hanging over the edge. Roll the remaining pastry into a circle large enough for the top and cut a 2-cm hole in the centre.

2. For the filling, heat the oil in a pan and cook the onion for 4 minutes until soft. Remove from heat and mix with 1/4 of the meats. Stir in the parsley and season to taste. Cover the base of the pastry with a layer of ham, then chicken. Cover with the parsley mix and add the remaining meat. Lay the pastry on top, trim the edges, then pinch the base and top edges together. Brush the top with half the beaten egg and cook for 45 minutes. (If it is browning too much, cover with foil.)

3. Remove the sides of the tin and brush the sides and top with egg. Bake for a further 15 minutes until golden brown. Remove from oven and leave to cool. Soak the gelatine leaves in cold water for 5 minutes. Squeeze out the excess water. Heat 60ml of the stock in a pan and stir in the gelatine until dissolved, then stir into the remaining stock. Leave to cool, but not set. Pour one-third of the stock into the cold pie, through the round hole in the top of the pastry a little at a time. Return the pie to the refrigerator for 15 minutes. Repeat with the rest of the jelly until used up.

Preparation time: 30 min
  plus 2 h 45 min chilling
Cooking time: 1 h
Serves 4

For the pastry:
375g plain flour
½ tsp salt
150ml water
130g lard

For the filling:
1 tbsp oil
1 onion, finely chopped
450g cooked ham, sliced
450g boneless, skinless chicken
  thighs, finely chopped
4 tbsp chopped parsley
3 gelatine leaves
300ml ham stock

To finish:
1 egg, beaten

Small red onion tarts

Preparation time: 20 min
plus 1 h chilling
Cooking time: 55 min
Serves 4

For the pastry:
450g plain flour
½ tsp salt
120g butter
1 egg yolk
120ml water

For the filling:
2 tbsp olive oil
4 red onions, thinly sliced
2 garlic cloves, crushed
2 tsp brown sugar
1 tbsp balsamic vinegar
1 tbsp chopped thyme
1 tbsp olive oil

To finish:
1 egg, beaten

To garnish:
salad leaves

1. For the pastry, sift the flour into a mixing bowl and stir in the salt. Rub in the butter until the mixture resembles breadcrumbs. Gradually add the egg yolk and water, a tablespoon at a time, mixing continuously until the mixture just comes together as a dough. (You may not need to use all of the water.) Roll the pastry into a ball, then wrap in cling film and chill for 1 hour.

2. Preheat the oven to 375°F (190°C). Grease 4 deep tart tins.

3. Heat the oil in a pan and cook the onions and garlic for 25–30 minutes until soft. Stir in the sugar, balsamic vinegar and thyme and leave to cool.

4. Roll out the pastry on a floured work surface, to fit the tins. Gently press the pastry into the tins, trimming off any excess, then prick the base of the pastry case several times with a fork. Brush the pastry cases with beaten egg.

5. Bake for 20–25 minutes until golden and crisp. Cool in the tins, then place on a wire rack to cool completely.

6. Spoon in the onion filling and garnish with salad leaves.

Crumble à la Provence

1. Heat the olive oil in a large frying pan and fry the onions and garlic for 5 minutes until softened.

2. Add the red pepper and fry for 5 minutes until softened, then stir in the tomatoes and thyme, and season with salt and black pepper. Stir in the olives.

3. Preheat the oven to 350°F (180°C). Grease a pie dish.

4. Put the vegetables into the pie dish.

5. For the crumble, put the flour in a mixing bowl and rub in the butter until the mixture is crumbly. Stir in the Parmesan and pine nuts and season with salt and pepper.

6. Sprinkle the crumble over the vegetables and bake for 25–30 minutes, until the top is golden and crisp.

Preparation time: 15 min
Cooking time: 45 min
Serves 4

For the filling:
4 tbsp olive oil
2 red onions, sliced
2 garlic cloves, crushed
1 red pepper, cut into strips
450g tomatoes, quartered
1 tbsp chopped thyme
200g black olives, pitted

For the crumble topping:
225g plain flour
110g cold butter
75g grated Parmesan cheese
50g pine nuts, toasted

Chocolate truffle tart

1. For the pastry, sift the flour and icing sugar into a mixing bowl. Rub in the butter until the mixture resembles breadcrumbs. Gradually add the water, a tablespoon at a time, mixing continuously until the mixture just comes together as a dough. (You may not need to use all of the water.) Roll the pastry into a ball, then wrap in cling film and chill for 1 hour.

2. Preheat the oven to 375°F (190°C). Line a 23cm flan or tart springform tin with non-stick baking paper.

3. Roll out the pastry on a floured surface and line the tin. Prick the pastry all over with a fork, line the pastry case with non-stick baking paper and fill it with rice or dried beans. Bake for 20 minutes until golden. Remove the paper and beans and cook for a further 5 minutes. Cool in the tin, then place on a wire rack to cool completely.

4. For the filling, put the plain chocolate, 2 tablespoons rum and 2 ½ tablespoons golden syrup in a heatproof bowl over a pan of simmering (not boiling) water and stir until melted. Remove the bowl and allow to cool slightly. Repeat the process with the milk chocolate and the remaining rum and golden syrup.

5. Whisk the cream lightly until it just holds its shape, and fold half into each the chocolate mixture. Pour the plain chocolate mixture into the pastry case and chill until set. Keep the milk chocolate mixture warm.

6. Pour over the milk chocolate mixture. Tap the tin to release any air bubbles and cover with cling film. Chill for several hours or overnight.

7. Place on a serving plate and dredge with sifted cocoa powder.

Preparation time: 20 min
plus 7 h chilling
Cooking time: 35 min
Serves 4–6

For the pastry:
225g plain flour
2 tbsp icing sugar
110g butter
2–3 tbsp water

For the filling:
225g dark chocolate, 70% cocoa
solids
4 tbsp dark rum
5 tbsp golden syrup
225g milk chocolate
600ml double cream
cocoa powder, to dust

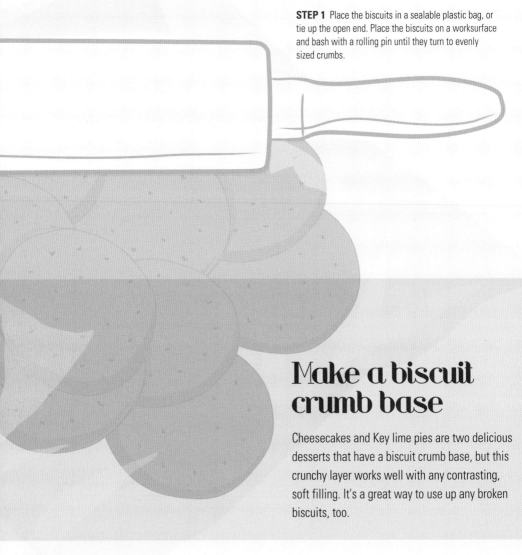

STEP 1 Place the biscuits in a sealable plastic bag, or tie up the open end. Place the biscuits on a worksurface and bash with a rolling pin until they turn to evenly sized crumbs.

Make a biscuit crumb base

Cheesecakes and Key lime pies are two delicious desserts that have a biscuit crumb base, but this crunchy layer works well with any contrasting, soft filling. It's a great way to use up any broken biscuits, too.

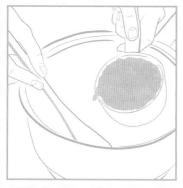

STEP 2 Tip out the crumbs into a large mixing bowl. Melt the butter in a saucepan and pour it into the biscuit crumbs, stirring well to combine.

STEP 3 Transfer the biscuit mixture to a springform tin. Using the back of a metal spoon, pack down the crumbs to an even layer. Chill until firm.

STEP 4 Once the base is firm, remove the tin from the fridge. Pour over the filling, according to your recipe, and smooth the top. Chill if needed.

STEP 5 Release the finished dessert from the tin, removing the sides and, using a spatula, the base before slicing, if you wish.

Mushroom pies

1. Preheat the oven to 400°F (200°C). Grease 4 individual soup bowls or dishes.

2. Heat the oil in a frying pan and add the onions, garlic and mushrooms. Cook gently until browned. Stir in the carrots, then add the stock. Bring to a boil, cover and simmer for about 10 minutes or until the carrots are tender.

3. Stir in the flour and simmer for 1–2 minutes, until the mixture has thickened. Remove from the heat and stir in the thyme. Season to taste with salt and pepper.

4. Spoon the mixture into the dishes and leave to cool.

5. Roll out the pastry and cut out 4 circles, a little larger than the tops of the dishes. Cut 1cm-thick strips to stick around the edge of the dishes, from the pastry trimmings.

6. Wet the edges of the pie dishes and stick the strips of pastry round the top edge. Wet the strips and stick a circle of pastry on top of each dish. Seal the edges and make 3 holes in the top of each pie with a fork.

7. Brush the tops with the beaten egg. Bake for 15–20 minutes until the pastry is golden brown and crisp. Sprinkle the pies with poppy seeds while hot.

Preparation time: 20 min
Cooking time: 40 min
Serves 4

2 tbsp olive oil
1 onion, finely chopped
1 garlic clove, finely chopped
125g large mushrooms, chopped
50g button mushrooms, quartered
1 carrot, diced
350ml vegetable stock
2 tbsp plain flour
1 tsp chopped thyme
500g puff pastry
1 egg, beaten

To garnish:
2 tbsp poppy seeds

Pear pie

1. Preheat the oven to 400°F (200°C). Grease 4 deep ramekins or bowls.

2. Divide the pastry into 4 and roll each piece into a circle larger than the pears. Reserve the pastry trimmings.

3. Mix the cardamom seeds and sugar and sprinkle on the pastry circles.

4. Put a pear upright on each pastry circle and brush the edges of the pastry with water and fold the pastry to come about three-quarters up around the pear. Put into the ramekins.

5. Roll out the pastry trimmings and cut 4 wide strips. Dampen the edges and attach to the edge of the ramekins.

6. Brush the pastry with beaten egg and sprinkle with the demerara sugar.

7. Bake for 30 minutes until the pastry is golden and the pears are soft.

Preparation time: 20 min
Cooking time: 30 min
Serves 4

500g puff pastry
4 ripe pears, peeled with stalks intact
1 tsp cardamom seeds, crushed
4 tbsp dark brown sugar
1 egg, beaten
3–4 tbsp demerara sugar

Chard tart

1. For the pastry, beat all the ingredients together in a mixing bowl to a smooth dough. Wrap in cling film and chill for 30 minutes.

2. Chop the chard stalks and tear the leaves into strips.

3. Heat 2 tablespoons oil in a pan and cook the chard, shallots and garlic for 3–4 minutes. Season with salt, pepper, nutmeg and lemon zest. Remove from the heat and cool slightly.

4. Heat the remaining oil in the pan and cook the mushrooms until browned. Tip into a bowl and stir in the chard, quark, crème fraîche, eggs and cheese mixing well. Season with salt, pepper and nutmeg.

5. Preheat the oven to 350°F (180°C). Grease a 23cm springform deep flan tin.

6. Roll out two-thirds of the pastry and line the tin. Spoon in the filling.

7. Roll out the remaining pastry to fit the top and place on top of the filling. Seal the edges well together and prick several times with a fork. Cut out leaves from the trimmings and attach to the pastry with beaten egg. Brush the pastry with the beaten egg.

8. Bake for 45–55 minutes until golden brown. Serve warm.

Preparation time: 25 min
  plus 30 min chilling
Cooking time: 1 h 10 min
Serves 4–6

For the pastry:
350g plain flour
175g butter, softened
a pinch of salt
1 egg, beaten
1–2 tbsp water

For the filling:
600g chard
4 tbsp olive oil
2 shallots, finely chopped
2 garlic cloves, finely chopped
grated nutmeg
½ tsp grated lemon zest
250g mushrooms, roughly chopped
400g quark
100ml crème fraîche
3 eggs
100g grated Gruyère cheese

To finish:
1 egg yolk, beaten

Mini chicken pot pies

Preparation time: 20 min
Cooking time: 35 min
Serves 8

For the filo cases:
75g butter, melted
270g filo pastry

For the filling:
40g butter
1 small onion, finely chopped
1 garlic clove, crushed
50g plain flour
450ml milk
250g cooked chicken, finely
  chopped
1 tbsp chopped thyme
3–4 tbsp cooked peas

To garnish:
thyme sprigs

1. Preheat the oven to 350°F (180°C). Grease an 8-hole muffin tin.

2. Cut the filo pastry into squares that are big enough to fit into the tins and hang over the sides a little. Brush each piece of filo with melted butter, then put a filo square into the tins and top with another filo square. Repeat with 3–4 pieces filo pastry for each tin, brushing each layer with melted butter.

3. Bake for 5–6 minutes until crisp and golden. Cool in the tins for 10 minutes.

4. For the filling, melt the butter in a pan and add the onion and garlic. Fry for 5–6 minutes, until translucent but not browned, then stir in the flour and cook for 2 minutes.

5. Gradually add the milk, stirring constantly and bring to the boil. Reduce the heat and simmer for 10–15 minutes, until thick and smooth, stirring occasionally. Season to taste with salt and black pepper, and fold in the chicken. Stir in the thyme and peas and leave to cool.

6. Remove the filo cases from the tins and spoon in the filling. Garnish with thyme and serve immediately.

Nut tart

1. For the pastry, sift the flour into a mixing bowl and stir in the salt. Rub in the butter until the mixture resembles breadcrumbs. Gradually add the water, a tablespoon at a time, mixing continuously until the mixture just comes together as a dough. Roll the pastry into a ball, then wrap in cling film and chill for 1 hour.

2. Preheat the oven to 375°F (190°C). Grease a rectangular tart tin.

3. Roll out the pastry on a floured surface and line the dish. Prick the pastry all over with a fork, line the pastry case with non-stick baking paper and fill it with rice or dried beans. Bake for 20 minutes. Remove the paper and beans.

4. For the filling, heat the sugar and water in a pan until the sugar has dissolved. Increase the heat and bring to a boil, without stirring, until the mixture is deep amber, swirling the pan occasionally.

5. Reduce the heat and gradually whisk in the cream (the mixture will bubble). Stir until smooth. Add the butter, honey and vanilla, then stir in the nuts.

6. Pour the mixture into the pastry case and bake for 20 minutes. Cool in the tin until the filling is set, then place on a wire rack to cool completely.

Preparation time: 20 min
  plus 1 h chilling
Cooking time: 50 min
Serves 4–6

For the pastry:
225g plain flour
½ tsp salt
110g butter
2–3 tbsp water

For the filling:
250g sugar
50ml water
150ml double cream
2 tbsp unsalted butter
1 tbsp honey
1 tsp vanilla extract
300g mixed nuts, coarsely chopped,
  e.g. walnuts, pecans, almonds,
  macadamias

Cappuccino tart

1. For the base, grind the sponge fingers in a food processor finely. Mix with the remaining ingredients for the base to form a dough. Wrap in cling film and chill for 1 hour.

2. Preheat the oven to 300°F (170°C). Butter a 28cm deep springform tart tin and press the base mixture over the bottom and sides of the tin.

3. For the filling, beat the butter and sugar until fluffy. Beat in the eggs, cheese, custard powder, baking powder, lemon zest and salt. Stir in the liqueur and vanilla seeds and paste.

4. Spoon the mixture onto the base and bake for 45 minutes until the filling is set.

5. Cool in the tin and remove when cold. Place a stencil on the top and sift over a thick layer of cocoa powder. Remove the stencil.

Preparation time: 15 min
plus 1 h chilling
Cooking time: 45 min
Serves 4–6

For the base:
100g sponge fingers
150g plain flour
1 tsp baking powder
110g butter
2 tsp instant coffee powder
1 tsp cocoa powder
1 egg white

For the filling:
70g butter
150g sugar
2 eggs
500g drained cottage cheese
½ packet custard powder
a pinch of baking powder
½ tsp grated lemon zest
a pinch of salt
4 tbsp almond liqueur
1 vanilla pod, seeds and paste
cocoa powder

Bakewell tart

1. For the pastry, put the flour, sugar, butter and egg yolks into a food processor and process at the highest setting until the mixture resembles breadcrumbs. Turn out onto a work surface and quickly combine to a smooth dough. Add 1–2 tbsp water if the pastry is too dry. Work in a little more flour if the pastry is too soft. Wrap in cling film and chill for 30 minutes.

2. Preheat the oven to 375°F (190°C). Grease a 23cm flan tin.

3. Roll out the pastry on a lightly floured surface and line the tin. Prick the pastry several times with a fork, cover with non-stick baking paper and baking beans and bake for 15 minutes. Remove the paper and beans. Reduce the oven temperature to 350°F (180°C).

4. For the filling, beat the sugar and butter until light, then gradually beat in the eggs until the mixture is pale and fluffy. Fold in the almond extract and ground almonds.

5. Spread the base of the pastry case with jam. Spread the mixture evenly over the jam and scatter with flaked almonds.

6. Bake for 30–40 minutes, until the filling is set and golden. Cover with tin foil if it browns too quickly. Sift over a little icing sugar while still hot. Leave to cool in the tin.

Preparation time: 20 min
plus 30 min
Cooking time: 1 h
Serves 4–6

For the pastry:
200g plain flour
2 tbsp icing sugar
100g butter
2 large egg yolks

For the filling:
150g sugar
150g butter
3 large eggs
½ tsp almond extract
150g ground almonds
4–6 tbsp raspberry jam
25g flaked almonds
2 tbsp icing sugar

Summer berry tart

Preparation time: 25 min
  plus 3 h 30 min chilling
Cooking time: 30 min
Serves 4–6

For the pastry:
175g plain flour
50g sugar
a pinch of salt
110g unsalted butter
1 large egg yolk
2–3 tbsp double cream

For the filling:
110g sugar
2 tbsp cornflour
450ml milk
1 large egg
2 large egg yolks
1 tsp vanilla extract
400g berries, e.g. raspberries,
* redcurrants, blueberries*
75g seedless raspberry or
* strawberry jam*

To decorate:
fresh flowers

1. For the pastry, mix together the flour, sugar, and salt in a mixing bowl. Rub in the butter until the mixture resembles breadcrumbs. Stir in the egg yolk and 2 tablespoons cream. Pour the egg mixture into the flour mixture and stir until the dough comes together and can be formed into a ball. If the pastry is too dry, add another tablespoon of cream. Shape into a ball, wrap in cling film and chill for 30 minutes.

2. Preheat the oven to 375°F (190°C). Grease a 25cm tart tin. Roll out the pastry on a floured surface and line the tin. Prick the pastry all over with a fork, line the pastry case with non-stick baking paper and fill it with rice or dried beans. Bake for 20–25 minutes until golden and cooked. Remove the paper and beans and leave to cool.

3. For the filling, put the sugar, cornflour and milk in a pan. Bring to a boil, stirring, and cook for 2 minutes. Whisk the egg and egg yolks until light. Pour about 1 cup of the hot milk mixture into the beaten eggs, whisking constantly.

4. Whisk the egg mixture into the hot milk in the pan and bring to a boil, whisking constantly. Remove from the heat and stir in the vanilla. Cover the surface with cling film, pressing it directly onto the top of the filling to prevent a skin forming. Cool, then chill for 3 hours until thickened.

5. Pour the chilled filling into the pastry case. Arrange the berries on top of the filling in a circular pattern.

6. Heat the jam in a small pan until melted. Remove from the heat. Brush the warm jam over the top of the fruit. Chill until ready to serve. Decorate with fresh flowers.

Tarte tatin

1. Heat the butter and sugar in an ovenproof frying pan until melted, stirring occasionally.

2. Remove the pan from the heat and arrange the apples in the pan, fitting them together tightly. Return the pan to the heat and bring to a boil.

3. Cook slowly for 20–40 minutes, depending on the ripeness of the fruit, until the mixture becomes caramel coloured. Remove from the heat and leave to cool.

4. Preheat the oven to 425°F (220°C).

5. Roll out the pastry 5cm larger than the pan and place it carefully over the apples, pressing the sides to the edges of the pan.

6. Bake for 20–25 minutes until the pastry is golden. Remove from the oven and leave to cool for 10 minutes. Run a knife around the edge of the pastry. Place a serving plate over the pan and invert onto the plate.

Preparation time: 20 min
Cooking time: 1 h 10 min
Serves 4

110g unsalted butter
200g caster sugar
8–10 apples, peeled, cored and
  quartered
300g puff pastry

Mixed berry tart

1. For the pastry, in a food processor, combine all the ingredients and process until the dough begins to come together. shape into a ball and wrap in cling film. Chill for 30 minutes.

2. Preheat the oven to 400°F (200°C). Butter 6 individual tart tins.

3. Divide the pastry into 6 equal pieces and press into the tins. Prick the pastry all over with a fork, line the pastry cases with non-stick baking paper and fill it with rice or dried beans. Bake for 20–25 minutes until golden and cooked. Remove the paper and beans and leave to cool.

4. For the filling, whisk the cream until thick and stir in the lemon curd until smooth. Spoon into the pastry cases.

5. Arrange the berries on top of the filling.

6. Warm the jam in a small pan and brush over the berries. Sift a little icing sugar over each tart.

Preparation time: 20 min
  plus 30 min chilling
Cooking time: 25 min
Serves 5

For the pastry:
200g plain flour
200g chilled unsalted butter, diced
1 large egg, beaten
2 tbsp sugar
1 tbsp double cream
2 tsp lemon juice
1 tsp salt

For the filling:
200ml double cream
200ml lemon curd
110g blackberries
200g sliced strawberries
6 tbsp seedless raspberry jam

To decorate:
icing sugar

Custard tart

1. For the pastry, put the flour in a mixing bowl and rub in the butter until the mixture resembles breadcrumbs. Add the caster sugar and egg yolk and mix to a dough. If it is too stiff add a little cold water. Wrap in cling film and chill for 20 minutes.

2. Preheat the oven to 350°F (180°C). Grease 4 small pie tins.

3. Roll out the pastry on a floured surface and line the tins.

4. For the filling, whisk the eggs lightly with the sugar. Heat the milk and cream until warm and pour on to the eggs, whisking lightly.

5. Strain through a sieve into the pastry cases and sprinkle with nutmeg, if using.

6. Bake for 20–25 minutes until the custard is set. Cool in the tins.

Preparation time: 20 min
   plus 20 min chilling
Cooking time: 25 min
Serves 4

For the pastry:
200g plain flour
100g butter
25g caster sugar
1 egg yolk

For the filling:
4 eggs
300ml milk
300ml double cream
110g sugar
grated nutmeg (optional)

Cherry tomato puff pastry tarts with basil

1. Heat the oil and butter in a frying pan and cook the onions, 12 tomatoes and garlic slowly for 20–30 minutes until caramelised. Add the balsamic vinegar and sugar, and cook for 2 minutes. Leave to cool.

2. Preheat the oven to 400°F (200°C). Grease a large baking tray.

3. Roll out the pastry to ½ cm thick. Cut out 4 x 15cm circles. Make a shallow cut in the puff pastry circles 1cm in from the edge and all the way around.

4. Spoon the tomato mixture into the centre of the pastry, leaving the cut edge clear.

5. Place the remaining tomatoes on top of the filling and scatter with the basil.

6. Brush the edges with beaten egg and bake for 20 minutes until the pastry is golden. Garnish with basil leaves.

Preparation time: 15 min
Cooking time: 50 min
Serves 4

1 tbsp olive oil
25g butter
4 red onions, chopped
24 cherry tomatoes, halved
1 garlic clove, finely chopped
1 tbsp balsamic vinegar
2 tbsp sugar
400g puff pastry
2 tbsp torn basil leaves
1 egg, beaten

To garnish:
basil leaves

Mini quiches with mushrooms, mozzarella and pine nuts

1. Preheat the oven to 400°F (200°C).

2. Grease a 12 hole muffin tin and scatter with breadcrumbs.

3. Heat the clarified butter in a pan and sweat the onions and garlic until translucent.

4. Turn up the heat, add the mushrooms and fry for a few minutes.

5. Turn the heat back down, season lightly with salt and pepper and continue frying until all the liquid has evaporated.

6. Beat together the quark, mozzarella, eggs, oatmeal and pine nuts until smooth and season with salt and pepper.

7. Drain the mushrooms if necessary and add to the quark mixture.

8. Spoon the mixture into the muffin pan and bake for around 20 minutes or until golden brown.

9. Remove from the oven, let cool for 5 minutes then remove carefully from the muffin pan.

10. Serve warm or cold, garnished with basil and pine nuts.

Preparation time: 20 min
Cooking time: 35 min
Serves 12

breadcrumbs
2–3 tbsp clarified butter
1 onion, finely chopped
1 garlic clove, finely chopped
200g mushrooms, chopped
100g oyster mushrooms, chopped
200g cep mushrooms, chopped
350g quark
200g mozzarella, finely chopped
4 eggs
3–4 tbsp oatmeal
50g chopped pine nuts

To garnish:
fresh basil, chopped into strips
2–3 tbsp pine nuts

Steak and ale pie

Preparation time: 25 min
  plus 2 h chilling
Cooking time: 1 h
Serves 4

For the pastry:
500g plain flour
250g butter
a pinch of salt
2 eggs
2 tbsp water

For the filling:
800g beef steaks, chopped into
  bite sized pieces
2 tbsp oil
3 stems thyme, leaves picked
2–3 tbsp plain flour
150ml ale
100g mushrooms, finely sliced

To finish:
1 egg yolk, beaten

1. For the pastry, sift the flour into a mixing bowl and make a well in the middle. Dot pieces of the butter, salt, eggs and water into the well. Knead quickly to a dough. Shape the dough into a ball, wrap in cling film and chill for 2 hours.

2. Preheat the oven to 400°F (200°C). Grease a large pie dish or tin.

3. Season the beef with salt and pepper. Heat the oil in a pan and fry the meat until brown all over. Add the thyme leaves.

4. Sprinkle the flour over the meat and pour over the ale. Bring to a boil and season with salt and pepper. Leave to cool. The sauce should be fairly thick. Mix in the mushrooms.

5. Roll out the pastry and cut out 2 circles. One should be large enough to cover the base of the pie dish. Line the pie dish with the larger circle and spoon on the meat and sauce. Cover with a pastry lid, pressing the edges down firmly. Decorate the edges if you wish, but make sure you cut a small hole in the top of the pie.

6. Brush the pie with beaten egg yolk and bake for 45 minutes until golden brown.

Orange pie

1. For the pastry, put the flour into a mixing bowl and stir in the butter, sugar, salt, egg and water. Mix with your hands to form a dough. Wrap in cling film and chill for 1 hour.

2. Preheat the oven to 350°F (180°C). Butter a deep flan tin or dish.

3. Roll out three-quarters of the pastry and line the flan tin.

4. For the filling, mix the butter, sugar, eggs, cornflour, crème fraîche and aniseed.

5. Put the cream mixture in the pastry base and cover with the orange segments. Spread with the orange marmalade.

6. Roll out the remaining pastry and cut into thin strips. Arrange on top of the filling in a lattice pattern.

7. Cut leaves out of the pastry trimmings and attach to the pastry with a little water.

8. Bake for 30–35 minutes until the pastry is golden.

Preparation time: 20 min
plus 1 h chilling
Cooking time: 35 min
Serves 4

For the pastry:
300g plain flour
150g butter, melted
50g sugar
a pinch of salt
1 egg, beaten
50ml water

For the filling:
50g butter, melted
50g icing sugar
2 eggs
2 tsp cornflour
300ml crème fraîche
1 tsp ground aniseed
6 oranges, peeled and segmented
5 tbsp orange marmalade, warmed

Strawberry cream pie

1. Butter a 20cm spring clip tin. Stir together the biscuit crumbs, melted butter and 2 tablespoons caster sugar. Press into the base of the tin and chill while you make the filling.

2. Arrange the strawberries on the biscuit base.

3. Beat the cream cheese with the remaining sugar and lemon juice.

4. Whisk the cream until thick and stir into the cream cheese mixture. Spoon carefully over the strawberries. Chill for at least 2 hours, until the filling is set.

Preparation time: 20 min
plus 2 h chilling
Serves 4

150g digestive biscuit crumbs
50g unsalted butter, melted
7 tbsp caster sugar
200g strawberries, halved
400g cream cheese
2 tbsp lemon juice
300ml double cream

Blueberry lime tart

1. For the pastry, sift the flour into a mixing bowl and rub in the butter until the mixture resembles breadcrumbs. Stir in the sugar and beat in the egg yolks. Gradually add the water, a tablespoon at a time, mixing continuously until the mixture just comes together as a dough. (You may not need to use all of the water.) Roll the pastry into a ball, then wrap in cling film and chill for 1 hour.

2. Preheat the oven to 350°F (180°C). Grease 4 x 10cm loose-based deep tart tins.

3. Roll out the pastry on a floured surface and line the tins. Prick the pastry all over with a fork, line the pastry cases with non-stick baking paper and fill with rice or dried beans. Bake for 10 minutes. Remove the paper and beans.

4. For the filling, mix together the sugar, cinnamon, cornflour, lime zest and juice and blueberries. Spoon into the pastry cases. Dot the butter on top.

5. For the crumble topping, put the flour into a bowl and rub in the butter until the mixture is crumbly. Stir in the sugar. Spoon on top of the filling.

6. Bake for 25–30 minutes until the crumble is golden brown. Cool in the tins.

Preparation time: 20 min
  plus 1 h chilling
Cooking time: 45 min
Serves 4

For the pastry:
225g plain flour
110g butter
50g caster sugar
2 egg yolks
2–3 tbsp water

For the filling:
50g sugar
½ tsp ground cinnamon
1 tsp cornflour
1 lime, finely grated zest and juice
110g blueberries
1 tbsp unsalted butter, diced

For the crumble topping:
110g self-raising flour
110g butter
110g sugar

Lemon blancmange and blueberry tart

Preparation time: 20 min
plus 2 h chilling
Cooking time: 45 min
Serves 4

For the pastry:
250g plain flour
½ tsp baking powder
3 tbsp fructose
a pinch of salt

For the filling:
250ml low-fat milk
2 tsp cornflour
2 tbsp water
2 egg yolks
2 tbsp grated lemon zest
sweetener
200g blueberries

1. For the pastry, mix all the ingredients with just enough water to form a smooth dough. Wrap in cling film and chill for 1 hour.

2. Preheat the oven to 350°F (180°C). Grease a baking dish.

3. Roll out the pastry on a lightly floured surface and line the baking dish. Prick the pastry all over with a fork, line the pastry with non-stick baking paper and fill with rice or dried beans. Bake for 30 minutes. Remove the paper and beans.

4. For the filling, heat the milk in a pan. Mix the cornflour with the water until smooth and stir into the milk. Bring to a boil and cook for 2 minutes. Stir in the egg yolks, lemon zest and sweetener to taste.

5. Pour into the pastry case and leave to cool. Place the blueberries on top of the filling and chill for at least 1 hour before serving.

Triple berry pie

1. For the pastry, sift the flour into a mixing bowl and stir in the sugar and salt. Rub in the butter until the mixture resembles breadcrumbs. Gradually add the egg and enough water until the mixture just comes together as a dough. Roll the pastry into a ball, then wrap in cling film and chill for 30 minutes.

2. Preheat the oven to 400°F (200°C). Grease a pie dish.

3. Sieve three-quarters of the berries and mash with the sugar, eggs and butter. Heat in a heatproof bowl over a pan of simmering water until well blended. Set aside to cool.

4. Roll out the pastry on a floured surface and line the dish. Line with non-stick baking paper and baking beans, and bake for 10 minutes. Reduce the oven temperature to 350°F (180°C) and bake for a further 20 minutes. Remove and leave to cool in the dish.

5. Spoon the berry purée into the pastry case and top with the remaining whole berries.

Preparation time: 20 min
plus 30 min chilling
Cooking time: 35 min
Serves 4

For the pastry:
250g plain flour
50g sugar
a pinch of salt
150g butter
1 egg

For the filling:
1kg mixed berries
100g sugar
3 eggs
70g butter

Pumpkin pie

1. For the pastry, sift the flour into a mixing bowl and stir in the salt. Rub in the butter until the mixture resembles breadcrumbs. Gradually add enough water until the mixture just comes together as a dough. Roll the pastry into a ball, then wrap in cling film and chill for 30 minutes.

2. Preheat the oven to 375°F (190°C). Grease a deep flan tin or dish.

3. Roll out the pastry on a floured work surface, until it is almost twice as wide as the diameter of the pie tin. Line the base and sides of the tin.

4. For the filling, place all the filling ingredients into a bowl and mix well. Pour into the pastry case.

5. Bake for about 45–50 minutes until the filling has set. Leave to cool and serve warm with whipped cream sprinkled with ground cinnamon.

Preparation time: 20 min
  plus 30 min chilling
Cooking time: 50 min
Serves 4

For the pastry:
225g plain flour
½ tsp salt
110g butter
2–3 tbsp water

For the filling:
225g fresh pumpkin purée, or 475g
  canned pumpkin
2 eggs, beaten
150ml double cream
75g dark brown sugar
1 tsp ground cinnamon
½ tsp ground ginger
a pinch of each, grated nutmeg,
  ground cloves, allspice

To serve:
whipped cream
ground cinnamon

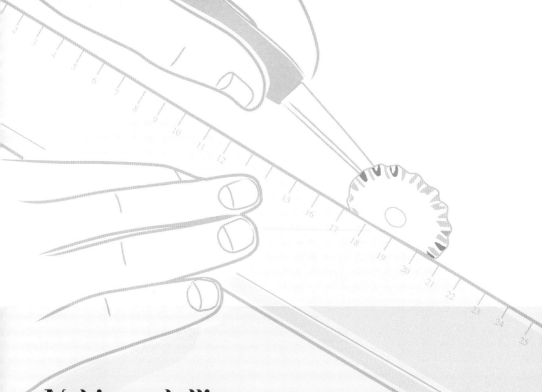

Making a lattice pie top

A pretty, lattice top makes a pie look homemade and adds a lovely decorative touch. Traditionally these tops are woven together, which is a little more fiddly than this, more simple, approach illustrated here.

STEP 1 Roll out the pastry for the pie lid to just beyond the diameter of the dish. Using a ruler to guide you, cut the pastry into even strips with a pastry wheel, if you have one, or a sharp knife.

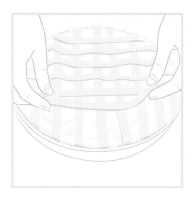

STEP 2 Place the filling into the pastry case, spreading the fruit evenly around the tin. Using a spoon, move stray bits of fruit to create a fairly smooth surface.

STEP 3 Carefully lay the pastry strips over the filling, going from one side to another. Turn the tin 90 degrees and lay strips to create a lattice effect.

STEP 4 When all the strips are neatly in place over the filling, crimp the ends of each into the side of the tin to seal them in place.

STEP 5 Beat an egg and, with a pastry brush, coat each of the pastry strips with the egg wash before placing the pie straight into the preheated oven.

Dark chocolate velvet pie

1. For the biscuit crumb, preheat the oven to 350°F (180°C). Line the base of a 20cm springform tin with non-stick baking paper.

2. Mix together the butter and biscuit crumbs. Stir in the pistachios. Press into the base and sides of the tin. Bake for 10 minutes and leave to cool before removing from the tin.

3. For the filling, put the sugar and water into a pan and heat gently until the sugar has dissolved. Bring to a boil and simmer without stirring until the mixture is a straw-coloured caramel.

4. Remove from the heat and stir in the butter and cream. Return to the heat and bring to a boil. Simmer for 10 minutes until thickened. Remove from the heat and add the chocolate, stirring until melted. Allow to cool a little.

5. Pour the cooled filling into the flan case and chill for about 2 hours until the filling has set. Decorate with strawberries, chocolate sprinkles and pistachios.

Preparation time: 20 min
 plus 2 h chilling
Cooking time: 25 min
Serves 4

For the biscuit crumb:
110g butter, melted
25g plain chocolate digestive
 biscuits, finely crushed
100g chopped pistachios

For the filling:
250g light brown sugar
150ml water
50g butter
150ml double cream
110g plain chocolate

To decorate:
halved strawberries
chocolate sprinkles
chopped pistachios

Coconut cream pie

1. For the pastry, mix the flour, butter and icing sugar together and pulse in a food processor until the ingredients are blended. Add the egg yolk, mix again and add enough water until the mixture forms a firm dough. Leave to rest for 10 minutes.

2. Preheat the oven to 350°F (180°C). Grease a 23cm springform flan tin or dish.

3. Roll out the pastry on a floured surface about 2mm thick. Line the tin with the pastry. Prick the base of the pastry case with a fork. Put a piece on non-stick baking parchment on the base of the pastry and weigh down with baking beans. Bake in the oven for 15–20 minutes until golden and cooked.

4. For the filling, mix together the sugar, cornflour, milk and 300 ml cream in a pan and heat, stirring. Bring to a boil and cook gently until the mixture is thick enough to coat the back of a spoon. Remove from the heat and whisk in the egg yolks, coconut and vanilla. Heat, stirring for 3 minutes until blended.

5. Remove the pastry case from the tin and place on a serving plate. Pour the coconut custard into the pastry case. Leave to cool, then chill for 2 hours until set.

6. Whisk the remaining cream until thick. Spread on top of the custard filling. Decorate with toasted flaked coconut and mint leaves.

Preparation time: 20 min
   plus 2 h chilling
Cooking time: 30 min
Serves 4

For the pastry:
250g plain flour
125g butter
100g icing sugar
1 egg yolk
50ml water

For the filling:
175g caster sugar
75g cornflour
220ml milk
600ml double cream
3 egg yolks
175g desiccated coconut
1 tsp vanilla extract

To decorate:
toasted flaked coconut
mint leaves

Apple berry pie

1. For the pastry, sift the flour into a mixing bowl and stir in the salt. Rub in the butter until the mixture resembles breadcrumbs. Gradually add the water, a tablespoon at a time, mixing continuously until the mixture just comes together as a dough. (You may not need to use all of the water.) Roll the pastry into a ball, then wrap in cling film and chill for 1 hour.

2. Preheat the oven to 400°F (200°C). Grease a 23cm pie dish.

3. Roll out half the pastry on a floured surface and line the pie dish.

4. Mix together the sugar, lemon juice and zest, and apple slices. Transfer to a pan with the butter and bring to a boil. Cook gently for 3 minutes until the apples are softened then add the berries and cook for 1 minute. Leave to cool.

5. Put the fruit into pie dish.

6. Roll out the remaining pastry on a floured surface, a little larger than the pie dish. Place on top of the filling. Seal the edges well and make a small hole in the top.

7. Brush the pastry lid with beaten egg, then dredge with caster sugar.

8. Bake for 20–25 minutes until the pastry is golden brown.

Preparation time: 20 min
    plus 1 h chilling
Cooking time: 35 min
Serves 4–6

For the pastry:
450g plain flour
1 tsp salt
225g butter
5–6 tbsp water

For the filling:
110g caster sugar
½ lemon, zest and juice
550g cooking apples, peeled, cored
    and thickly sliced
25g butter
150g mixed berries, e.g. raspberries,
    blackberries

To finish:
1 egg, beaten
caster sugar

Lemon meringue pie

Preparation time: 25 min
  plus 1 h chilling
Cooking time: 1 h 10 min
Serves 4

For the pastry:
225g plain flour
½ tsp salt
110g butter
2–3 tbsp water

For the filling:
200g caster sugar
2 lemons, finely grated, zest and
  juice
1 egg yolk, beaten
1 tbsp cornflour, mixed with a
  little milk
175ml boiling water

For the meringue topping:
2 egg whites
75g caster sugar

1. For the pastry, sift the flour into a mixing bowl and stir in the salt. Rub in the butter until the mixture resembles breadcrumbs. Gradually add the water, a tablespoon at a time, mixing continuously until the mixture just comes together as a dough. Roll the pastry into a ball, then wrap in cling film and chill for 1 hour.

2. Preheat the oven to 400°F (200°C). Grease a pie dish. Roll out the pastry on a floured work surface and line the dish. Prick the base of the pastry case several times with a fork. Cover the pastry with a sheet of non-stick baking paper and fill it with rice or dried beans. Bake for 15 minutes, until the pastry is pale golden. Remove from the oven and remove the beans and paper. Reduce the oven temperature to 300°F (150°C).

3. For the filling, put the sugar, and the lemon zest and juice into a pan. Mix the egg yolk with the cornflour mixture, then add to the pan with the boiling water. Bring to a boil, stirring, then simmer over a low heat, stirring constantly, until thickened. Remove from the heat and allow to cool. Pour the cooled filling into the pastry case in the dish.

4. For the meringue topping, whisk the egg whites until stiff peaks form. Whisk in 1 tablespoon of sugar, then add the remaining sugar, 1 tablespoon at a time, whisking constantly. Spread the meringue topping over the pie filling and bake for 45–50 minutes, until the meringue is light golden and crisp on the outside, but soft underneath. Serve warm or cold.

Black bottom pie

1. For the biscuit crumb, preheat the oven to 350°F (180°C). Line the base of a 20cm deep springform tin with non-stick baking paper.

2. Mix together the butter and biscuit crumbs. Press into the base and sides of the tin. Bake for 10 minutes and leave to cool before removing from the tin.

3. For the chocolate layer, put the chocolate, marshmallows and water into a heatproof bowl over a pan of simmering (not boiling) water until the mixture melts. Cool slightly.

4. Stir the egg yolk into the chocolate mixture and leave until cold.

5. Whisk the double cream until it forms soft peaks. Whisk the egg white until stiff and fold it carefully into the chocolate mixture together with the cream. Turn into the biscuit case and chill for 1 hour until set.

6. For the custard layer, whisk the eggs and sugar with an electric whisk until blended. Stir in the butter and lemon juice and pour into a pan.

7. Heat, stirring, and bring to a boil. Remove from the heat and allow to cool. Pour over the set chocolate layer and chill for 1 hour.

8. For the topping, whisk the cream until thick and spread over the custard layer. Chill until ready to serve.

Preparation time: 20 min
  plus 1 h chilling
Cooking time: 20 min
Serves 4

For the biscuit crumb:
110g butter, melted
25 plain chocolate digestive biscuits,
  finely crushed

For the chocolate layer:
100g plain chocolate
15 marshmallows
2 tbsp water
1 egg, separated
150ml double cream

For the custard layer:
4 eggs
110g sugar
175g butter, diced
110ml lemon juice

For the topping:
300ml double cream

Cherry pie

1. For the filling, toss the cherries and sugar together with the kirsch and leave to stand for 30 minutes.

2. For the pastry, put the flour in a mixing bowl and rub in the butter until the mixture resembles breadcrumbs. Add the caster sugar and egg yolks and mix to a dough. If it is too stiff add a little cold water. Wrap in cling film and chill for 20 minutes.

3. Preheat the oven to 375°F (190°C). Grease a large pie dish.

4. Roll out half the pastry and line the pie dish. Put the cherry mixture in the dish.

5. Roll out the remaining pastry and cut out a lattice pattern with a sharp knife or lattice cutter. Place on top of the pie and crimp and seal the edges. Brush with beaten egg.

6. Bake for 30–35 minutes until the pastry is crisp and golden.

Preparation time: 20 min
plus 30 min soaking and
20 min chilling
Cooking time: 35 min
Serves 4

For the filling:
500g cherries, pitted
3 tbsp sugar
1 tbsp kirsch

For the pastry:
400g plain flour
200g butter
50g caster sugar
2 egg yolks

To finish:
1 egg, beaten

Berry pie

1. Preheat the oven to 350°F (180°C). Line a baking tray with non-stick baking paper.

2. Beat together the butter and icing sugar in a mixing bowl until creamy.

3. Add the flour and salt and work together to form a stiff dough, then knead lightly for a few moments until smooth.

4. Pat or roll out the dough into a circle, with a thickness of about 1cm. Cut into 8 wedges. Brush with the egg white and sprinkle with the caster sugar.

5. Place on the baking tray and bake for 12–15 minutes until pale golden. Cool the biscuits for a few minutes on the tray, then place on a wire rack to cool completely.

6. Preheat the oven to 350°F (180°C). Grease a baking dish.

7. Mix the berries, sugar and cornflour and put into the baking dish. Cook for 25–30 minutes until the berries are soft. Leave to cool.

8. Place the biscuits on top of the dish and decorate with whole berries. Serve with vanilla ice cream.

Preparation time: 20 min
Cooking time: 45 min
Serves 4

For the biscuits:
225g unsalted butter
110g icing sugar
375g plain flour
a pinch of salt
1 egg white, lightly beaten
50g caster sugar

For the filling:
450g mixed berries, e.g. raspberries,
*   blueberries*
110g sugar
2 tbsp cornflour

To decorate:
whole berries

Shepherds pie

Preparation time: 20 min
Cooking time: 55 min
Serves 4

300g potatoes, peeled
2 tbsp oil
2 onions, finely chopped
400g minced lamb
1 tsp tomato purée
40ml hot milk
grated nutmeg
50g Cheddar cheese, grated

1. Preheat the oven to 400°F (200°C). Butter 4 small oven-proof bowls or souffle dishes 250 ml capacity, or 1 large dish 1 litre capacity.

2. Cook the potatoes in boiling salted water for 25 minutes or until tender.

3. Heat the oil and fry the onions until translucent, then add the meat and cook for about 10 minutes. Add the tomato purée and season with salt and pepper.

4. Drain and mash the potatoes. Stir in the hot milk and season with salt, pepper and nutmeg.

5. Spoon the meat mixture into the bowls, top with the mashed potato and sprinkle with cheese. Bake for about 20 minutes until golden brown.

Steak and kidney pudding

1. For the suet crust, sift the flour and the salt into a mixing bowl and mix. Add just enough water to form a soft dough.

2. Roll out the pastry on a lightly floured surface into a round disc approximately 1cm thick. Cut out a quarter of the dough for the lid and set aside.

3. Use the remainder of the pastry to line a well buttered 1.75 litre pudding basin, leaving at least 1cm of the dough hanging over the edge.

4. For the filling, toss the steak and kidney in the flour, salt and pepper. Spoon into the lined pudding basin. Do not push the meat filling into the basin. Add the beef stock to come nearly two-thirds to the top, not covering the meat completely.

5. Place the pastry lid over the filling and fold the border over. Press the pastry together securely to seal.

6. Cover the pudding with a double piece of buttered foil, pleated in the middle. Tie in place with string.

7. Steam the pudding on an upturned plate in a large pan filled with boiling water for 5 hours, topping up with boiling water occasionally so the pan doesn't boil dry.

8. Turn out the pudding onto a large warm serving plate.

Preparation time: 30 min
Cooking time: 5 h 25 min
Serves 4

For the suet crust:
450g self-raising flour
225g shredded suet
1 tsp salt

For the filling:
675g stewing steak, cubed
225g ox kidney, cubed
2 tbsp plain flour
150ml beef stock

Plum pie

1. For the pastry, sift the flour into a mixing bowl and stir in the sugar. Rub in the butter until the mixture resembles breadcrumbs. Gradually add the egg and lemon zest until the mixture just comes together as a dough. You may need to add a little water. Roll the dough into a ball, then wrap in cling film and chill for 20 minutes.

2. Make the topping next, mix all the ingredients together until well blended. Chill for 30 minutes.

3. Preheat the oven to 350°F (180°C). Grease a 28cm pie dish or tin.

4. Roll out the dough on a floured work surface, until it is almost twice as wide as the diameter of the pie tin. Line the base and sides of the tin.

5. For the filling, spread the jam over the base of the pastry case, cover with the plums and sprinkle with icing sugar and cinnamon. Put spoonfuls of the chilled topping on top of the plums.

6. Bake for 40–50 minutes until the topping is golden and the pastry is browned. Sprinkle with caster sugar while hot.

Preparation time: 30 min
    plus 50 min chilling
Cooking time: 50 min
Serves 4–6

For the pastry:
250g plain flour
100g icing sugar
125g butter
1 egg, beaten
1 lemon, finely grated zest

For the filling:
6 tbsp plum jam
450g plums, pitted and quartered
50g icing sugar
½ tsp ground cinnamon

For the topping:
250g ground almonds
50g plain flour
½ tsp almond extract
250g unsalted butter, melted
250g caster sugar
3 eggs, beaten

To finish:
caster sugar

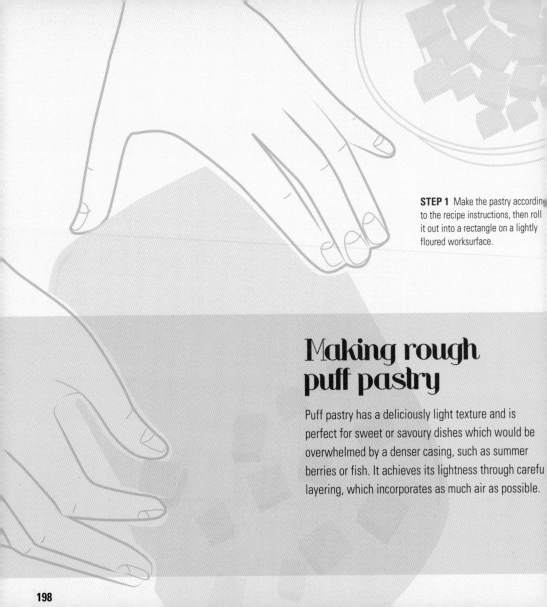

STEP 1 Make the pastry according to the recipe instructions, then roll it out into a rectangle on a lightly floured worksurface.

Making rough puff pastry

Puff pastry has a deliciously light texture and is perfect for sweet or savoury dishes which would be overwhelmed by a denser casing, such as summer berries or fish. It achieves its lightness through careful layering, which incorporates as much air as possible.

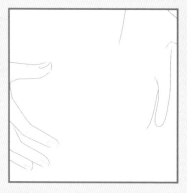

STEP 2 Evenly scatter small pieces of butter over the rectangle of pastry. Fold over the top third of the rectangle to cover the butter.

STEP 3 Fold over the lower third of the pastry to create a rectangle. Roll out from the short end until the pastry is three times its original length.

STEP 4 Chill the pastry for 20 minutes then roll it out to the size and shape you require. Gently position the pastry lid in place and crimp the edges.

STEP 5 Once the pastry lid is in place, go around the outside of the pie plate and trim the pastry, using a sharp knife, to create a neat finish.

Chocolate cherry tart

1. For the pastry, sift the flour into a mixing bowl and stir in the salt. Rub in the butter until the mixture resembles breadcrumbs. Gradually add the water, a tablespoon at a time, mixing continuously until the mixture just comes together as a dough. Roll the dough into a ball, then wrap in cling film and chill for 1 hour.

2. Preheat the oven to 375°F (190°C). Grease a 23cm deep flan or tart tin. Roll out the pastry on a floured surface and line the tin. Prick the pastry all over with a fork, line the pastry case with non-stick baking paper and fill it with rice or dried beans. Bake for 20 minutes until golden and cooked. Remove the paper and beans and leave to cool.

3. For the filling, melt the chocolate in a heatproof bowl over a pan of simmering (not boiling) water. Leave to cool. Stir 100ml cream into the chocolate. Whisk the egg yolks with 50g sugar, then add to the chocolate. Whisk the egg whites with the remaining sugar until stiff. Fold into the chocolate mixture. Whisk the remaining cream until thick and stir in the kirsch. Fold into the chocolate mixture. Spread the jam over the base of the pastry base. Pour the chocolate filling on top and chill for 2 hours.

4. For the poached cherries: place the cherries, red wine, kirsch, sugar and lemon juice in a pan and bring to a boil. Simmer for 2–3 minutes until the cherries are tender. Using a slotted spoon, remove the cherries from the liquid and set aside. Bring the liquid back to a boil. Cook for 4–5 minutes until syrupy. Pour the syrup over the cherries, reserving 4 tablespoons and set aside to cool.

5. For the cherry cream: whisk the cream thick. Stir in the reserved cherry syrup, to give a marbled effect. Place the poached cherries on the filling and a swirl of cherry cream.

Preparation time: 30 min
  plus 3 h chilling
Cooking time: 30 min
Serves 4–6

For the pastry:
225g plain flour
½ tsp salt
110g butter
2–3 tbsp water

For the filling:
400g plain chocolate, 70% cocoa
  solids
400ml double cream
5 eggs, separated
100g sugar
1 tbsp kirsch
175g cherry jam

For the poached cherries:
250g cherries, pitted
250ml red wine
1 tbsp kirsch
75g sugar
½ lemon, juice

For the cherry cream:
300ml double cream
4 tbsp cherry syrup

Meat pie with duck liver and truffle in puff pastry

1. Marinate the duck and pork in the orange juice, port and Grand Marnier for 1 hour.

2. Heat the oil in a frying pan and add the duck liver, bay leaf, peppercorns and shallots and fry briefly. Pour in the cognac, water and red wine. Simmer for 30 minutes. Stir in the thyme.

3. Purée half the pork and duck mixture in a food processor.

4. Mix the orange zest, spices, pistachios and eggs with the puréed mixture and the remaining meat cubes. Season with salt and pepper.

5. Preheat the oven to 425°F (220°C). Grease a terrine or loaf tin.

6. Roll out the pastry and use two-thirds to line the tin.

7. Spoon in half the meat mixture. Place the truffle pieces down the centre. Cover evenly with the remaining meat mixture. Cover the meat with the remaining pastry and pierce 3 holes in the lid.

8. Brush with beaten egg and bake for 10 minutes, then reduce the oven temperature to 350°F (180°C) and bake for a further 40–60 minutes until the pastry is golden brown and the filling is cooked. Cover with foil if the pastry is browning too quickly.

Preparation time: 30 min
  plus 1 h marinating
Cooking time: 1 h 45 min
Serves 4

900g duck breast meat, cubed
200g pork fillet, cubed
250g pork fat, diced
2 tbsp port
½ orange, zest and juice
1 tbsp Grand Marnier
2 tbsp oil
1 duck liver
1 bay leaf
6 peppercorns
2 shallots, chopped
2 tbsp Cognac
1 litre water
250ml red wine
1 tsp chopped thyme
1 tsp ground ginger
¼ tsp ground cloves
½ tsp grated nutmeg
80g pistachios
2 eggs
100g black truffle, chopped
500g puff pastry

To finish:
1 egg, beaten

Damson crumble tart

1. For the pastry, sift the flour into a mixing bowl and stir in the sugar. Rub in the butter until the mixture resembles breadcrumbs. Gradually add the water, a tablespoon at a time, mixing continuously until the mixture just comes together as a dough. (You may not need to use all of the water.) Roll the dough into a ball, then wrap in cling film and chill for 1 hour.

2. Preheat the oven to 375°F (190°C).

3. Roll out the pastry on a floured surface and line the base and sides of the tin.

4. Mix together the damsons and sugar and put into the pastry case. Bake for 15 minutes.

5. For the topping, mix all the ingredients together with a fork until combined. Place spoonfuls of the topping on the filling and bake for a further 15 minutes, until the damsons are soft and the pastry is golden. Cool in the tin.

Preparation time: 15 min
  plus 1 h chilling
Cooking time: 30 min
Serves 4–6

For the pastry:
225g plain flour
1 tbsp sugar
110g butter
2–3 tbsp water

For the filling:
700g damsons, pitted
110g light brown sugar

For the topping:
175g ground almonds
1 lemon, finely grated zest
6 tsp honey
4 tsp butter
1 tsp vanilla extract

White chocolate tartlets

Preparation time: 30 min
  plus 3 h cooling and chilling
Cooking time: 45 min
Serves 4

For the pastry:
100g plain flour
A pinch of salt
50g butter
1 tbsp caster sugar
1 egg yolk

For the filling:
250ml double cream
125g white chocolate, broken into
  pieces
½ vanilla pod, seeds only
1 egg, separated
Raspberries and shards white
  chocolate, to decorate

1. To make the pastry, sift the flour and salt into a mixing bowl. Rub in the butter using your fingertips until the mixture resembles breadcrumbs. Stir in the sugar until well combined. Stir in the egg yolk and 2 tablespoons cold water until the mixture forms a firm dough. Knead lightly on a floured work surface. Cover with clear film and chill for 30 minutes.

2. Roll the pastry out on a lightly floured work surface and use to line 4 x 3cm deep, 9cm round, loose bottomed, fluted tartlet tins. Prick the base and sides with a fork, cover and chill for 30 minutes. Meanwhile, preheat the oven to 375°F (190°C).

3. Line the pastry cases with baking parchment and baking beans and bake blind for 10 minutes. Remove the beans and paper and bake for a further 5 minutes. Remove from the heat.

4. Reduce the oven temperature to 325°F (160°C). For the filling, melt together the cream and chocolate, stirring occasionally, until smooth. Remove from the heat and allow to cool.

5. Stir the vanilla seeds and egg yolk into chocolate mixture. Whisk the egg white in a large bowl until soft peaking and then fold in chocolate mixture until well combined. Pour into the prepared pastry cases and bake for about 20–25 minutes, until the filling is set. Allow to cool and chill for 2 hours. Decorate with raspberries and shards of white chocolate.

Onion tart

1. To make the pastry, sift the flour and salt into a mixing bowl. Rub in the butter using your fingertips until the mixture resembles breadcrumbs. Stir in the egg yolk and 3–4 tablespoons cold water until the mixture forms a firm dough. Knead lightly on a floured work surface. Cover with clear film and chill for 30 minutes.

2. Roll the pastry out on a lightly floured work surface and use to line a 23cm, round, loose bottomed, fluted flan tin. Chill for 30 minutes. Preheat the oven to 375°F (190°C).

3. Line the pastry case with baking parchment and baking beans, and bake blind for 10 minutes. Remove the beans and paper and bake for a further 10 minutes. Remove from the heat and reduce the oven temperature to 350°F (180°C).

4. Meanwhile, to make the filling, melt the butter in a large pan. Add the onions and seasoning, and sauté over a very low heat for about 45 minutes, stirring occasionally until softened. Remove from the heat and stir in the thyme.

5. Spread the mustard over the base of the flan. Scatter over half the cheese. Beat together the crème fraîche, eggs and remaining cheese. Stir in the onions and pour into the pastry case. Bake for 45–55 minutes, until golden.

Preparation time: 30 min
   plus 1 h cooling and chilling
Cooking time: 1 h 45 min
Serves 6

For the pastry:
175g plain flour
a pinch of salt
75g butter

For the filling:
50g butter
4 large white onions, halved and sliced
1½ tbsp fresh chopped thyme
2 tbsp Dijon mustard
150g Gruyere cheese, grated
300ml crème fraîche
2 eggs, beaten

Fish pie

1. Preheat the oven to 375°F (190°C). Cook the potatoes in a large pan of boiling water for 15–20 minutes, until tender. Drain and return to the pan. Turn down the heat, add the butter and milk and bring to the boil. Remove from the heat, season and, using an electric whisk, beat until smooth. Cover and set aside.

2. Meanwhile, place the eggs in a pan of water, bring to the boil and simmer for 7 minutes, until hard boiled. Drain and place in a bowl of cold water until cool. Remove the shells.

3. Bring the wine to the boil in a saucepan and boil rapidly until reduced by half. Add the cream and boil rapidly until reduced and thickened. Arrange the fish in the base of a ovenproof dish. Season the sauce and stir in chives. Pour over the fish evenly.

4. Cut the eggs into quarters and arrange on top of the fish. Spread over the mashed potatoes creating a fluffy effect. Scatter over the cheese and bake for 30 minutes, until the top is golden.

Preparation time: 20 min
Cooking time: 1 h
Serves 4

1kg potatoes
50g butter
4 tbsp whole milk
3 eggs
450ml white wine
400ml double cream
425g salmon fillet, skinned and cut into large pieces, thawed if frozen
275g undyed smoked haddock fillet, skinned and cut into large pieces, thawed if frozen
240g cooked and peeled jumbo king prawns, thawed if frozen
2 tbsp fresh chopped chives
100g Cheddar cheese, grated

Cottage pie

1. Preheat the oven to 375°F (190°C). Heat a large pan and fry the mince for about 8 minutes, stirring occasionally and breaking up any lumps, until browned.

2. Add the onions, celery and carrots and cook for 5 minutes, stirring occasionally. Stir in the remaining ingredients and bring to the boil. Cover and simmer for 30 minutes, stirring occasionally. Uncover and simmer for a further 20 minutes.

3. Meanwhile, cook the potatoes and parsnips together in a large pan of boiling water for 20 minutes, until tender. Drain and return to the pan. Turn down the heat, add the nutmeg, butter and milk and bring to the boil. Remove from the heat, season, and using an electric whisk, beat until smooth. Cover and set aside.

4. Spoon the meat sauce into an ovenproof dish and top with the mash. Rough up with a fork and scatter over the cheese. Bake for 30–35 minutes, until the mash is golden.

Preparation time: 20 min
Cooking time: 1 h 40 min
Serves 4

500g minced beef
2 onions, chopped
2 sticks celery, sliced
2 medium carrots, diced
1 tbsp fresh thyme leaves
2 tbsp tomato puree
300ml good beef stock
2 tbsp Worcestershire sauce

For the mash:
750g potatoes, cut into medium size pieces
250g parsnips, cut into medium size pieces
A pinch of freshly grated nutmeg
25g butter
6 tbsp whole milk
50g freshly grated Parmesan

Turkey, ham and leek pie

Preparation time: 20 min
 plus 20 min chilling
Cooking time: 50 min
Serves 4

50g butter
4 medium leeks, thickly sliced
1 garlic clove
1 tsp English mustard powder
2 tbsp plain flour
325ml chicken stock
4 tbsp double cream
2 tbsp fresh chopped mixed herbs
300g cooked turkey, cut into bite-
 size pieces
300g good-quality cooked ham,
 cut into bite size pieces
375g packet ready rolled puff
 pastry
1 egg, whisked

1. Heat the butter in a large pan and cook the leeks and garlic for 5–10 minutes, until softened. Stir in the mustard and flour and cook for 2 minutes, stirring constantly. Remove the pan from the heat and gradually blend in the stock and cream.

2. Return the pan to the heat and bring to the boil, stirring until thickened. Season to taste. Stir in the herbs, turkey and ham. Spoon into a pie dish and set aside.

3. Unroll the pastry out on a lightly floured work surface and cut a piece large enough to cover the pie. Brush the edges of the pie dish with water. Cut a strip of pastry from the trimmings and lay on the edge of the dish. Brush with water and top with the cut sheet of pastry pressing pastry together to seal. Trim, and using a sharp knife, knock up the edges. Cut a steam in the centre of the pie. Cover and chill for 20 minutes.

4. Preheat the oven to 425°F (220°C). Brush the pastry with beaten egg and bake for 30–35 minutes, until well risen and golden.

Raspberry meringue pie

1. Heat the oven to 310°F (160°C). Grease a pie dish.

2. Mix the flour and salt together in a mixing bowl and rub in the butter, until the mixture resembles breadcrumbs. Add the water a tablespoon at a time and mix to a dough.

3. Roll out the dough on a floured surface to a thickness of 3mm. Line the pie dish. Prick the base and sides with a fork and line with greaseproof paper, and fill with baking beans. Bake for 10–15 minutes. until pale golden. Remove the paper and beans. Cool in the dish.

4. For the filling, blend the raspberries to a pulp and sieve the juices into a pan.

5. Mix the cornflour, sugar, lemon juice and water to form a paste. Pour the paste into the raspberry purée and bring to a boil over a medium heat. Reduce the heat and simmer, stirring constantly for 1 minute until the mixture has thickened. Add more sugar to taste. Set aside to cool slightly.

6. Stir in the egg yolks and butter, and leave to cool further before pouring into the pastry case. Chill for 30 minutes.

7. Increase the oven temperature to 350°F (180°C).

8. For the meringue, whisk the egg whites until stiff. Add the sugar to the mixture a spoonful at a time, whisking continuously.

9. Spread the meringue on top of the chilled pie filling and cook for about 10 minutes, until the meringue is golden.

Preparation time:
Cooking time: 35 min
   with 30 min for chilling
Serves 4–6

For the pastry:
250g plain flour
¼ tsp salt
110g unsalted butter
2–3 tbsp cold water

For the filling:
800g raspberries
5 tbsp cornflour
110g sugar
2 tbsp lemon juice
2 tbsp water
5 large egg yolks
50g butter

For the meringue:
4 egg whites
200g caster sugar

Mud pie

1. For the pastry, sift the flour and cocoa powder into a mixing bowl. Rub in the butter until the mixture resembles breadcrumbs. Stir in the sugar and enough water to form a soft dough.

2. Wrap the dough in cling film and chill for 15 minutes.

3. Heat the oven to 375°F (190°C). Grease a 23cm springform flan tin.

4. Line the tin with the dough, pressing it into the base and sides. Line the dough with baking paper and baking beans. Bake 'blind' for 15 minutes. Remove the beans and paper and cook for a further 10 minutes until crisp. Reduce the oven temperature to 310°F (160°C).

5. For the filling, whisk the butter and sugar in a mixing bowl and gradually whisk in the eggs and cocoa powder. Beat in the chocolate and coffee, followed by the cream. Pour the mixture into the pastry case and bake for 30–40 minutes until set. Cool in the tin for 10 minutes, then remove from the tin and place on a wire rack to cool completely. Chill for at least 1 hour.

6. For the topping, whisk the cream until thick and put into a piping bag. Pipe on top of the chilled filling and drizzle with the melted chocolate.

Preparation time:
Cooking time: 1 h 20 min
  with 1 h 15 min for chilling
Serves 4–6

For the pastry:
225g plain flour
25g cocoa powder
150g butter
1 tbsp sugar
2 tbsp water

For the filling:
175g butter
4 eggs, lightly whisked
4 tbsp cocoa powder
175g dark brown sugar
175g dark chocolate, 70% cocoa
  solids; melted
2 tsp coffee granules
300ml double cream

For the topping:
300ml double cream
110g dark chocolate,
  melted

INDEX

Notes

Notes

Notes

Notes

Notes

Notes

Favourite recipes

Favourite recipes

Favourite recipes

Favourite recipes

Favourite recipes